The Shakespeare Revue

First presented by the RSC at the Barbican Centre and subsequently in the West End, this popular anthology gathers together some of the finest comic material inspired by Shakespeare. Incorporating many specially commissioned items, it is delightfully illustrated by leading theatre caricaturists, cartoonists and designers.

CHRISTOPHER LUSCOMBE began his career writing and performing for the Footlights Revue at Cambridge. He worked extensively in rep before appearing at the Old Vic in *Kean*, and then joined the Royal Shakespeare Company, with whom he has spent the last five years. His many roles have included Dapper in *The Alchemist*, Vasya in *Artists and Admirers*, Moth in *Love's Labour's Lost* and Launcelot Gobbo in *The Merchant of Venice*. His one-man show *Half Time*, co-written with Richard Bonneville, has been seen at the Bush Theatre, the Donmar Warehouse and on tour.

MALCOLM McKEE has played leading roles in theatres all over the country – Sir Benjamin Backbite in *The School for Scandal*, Mephistophiles in *Doctor Faustus*, Trinculo in *The Tempest* and the Dentist in *Little Shop of Horrors*. He has devised a number of revues – *The Cocktail Hour, End of Term, Theatrical Digs* – and composed scores for many plays and musicals in the theatre, including *A Midsummer Night's Dream, The Tempest* and *Torch Song Trilogy*. For radio his scores include *Tom and Viv, The Country Wife, Time and the Conways* and *Some Tame Gazelle* plus the music and lyrics for *The Good Companions*. Other writing includes a new adaptation of *Oh, What a Lovely War!* for Radio 3. He also works as a freelance graphic designer.

THE
Shakespeare
REVUE

compiled by

CHRISTOPHER LUSCOMBE

and

MALCOLM McKEE

with a foreword by

ADRIAN NOBLE

NICK HERN BOOKS

London

A Nick Hern Book

The Shakespeare Revue first published in Great Britain in 1994 as a paperback original by Nick Hern Books Limited, 14 Larden Road, London W3 7ST

This revised edition published in 1995.

Typeset by Country Setting, Woodchurch, Kent TN26 3TB

Printed in Great Britain by Cox and Wyman Ltd, Reading, Berks

A catalogue record for this book is available from the British Library

ISBN 1 85459 259 9

For
Carol, Kathy,
Sonja and Wayne

Contents

Illustrations

Foreword

I have always regarded comedy as a deeply serious art, and approached masters of the craft with considerable awe. They possess meticulous technique, cunningly disguised in a relaxed spontaneity; the results of their efforts are immediately and cruelly manifest – the audience either laugh or they don't. Small wonder then that the lunchtime hubub in the green room of the Bristol Old Vic when I started out as a director in the late seventies was always sharply divided: unrestrained hysteria and mirth from the actors rehearsing the tragedy and intense, urgent negotiations amongst those working on the comedy.

Christopher Luscombe and Malcolm McKee have compiled a revue, one of the trickiest and most elusive forms of comic entertainment. They have no storyline to support them; the art requires almost limitless gifts of characterisation, intellectual dexterity, versatility, lightness and delicacy of touch, precision. In other words, wit. The Elizabethans, of course, put a high price on wit – that ability to stimulate our intelligence while making us laugh – and regarded it as the natural accompaniment to all aspects of a civilised adult life.

Chris and Malcolm's *Shakespeare Revue* celebrates Shakespeare by showing us his reflection in the ink of dozens of authors and wits. Falstaff boasts 'I am not only witty in myself, but the cause that wit is in other men.' *The Shakespeare Revue* spectacularly applies the same maxim to Shakespeare and succeeds in full measure.

ADRIAN NOBLE
Artistic Director, RSC

Introduction

The idea for *The Shakespeare Revue* came about
on Shakespeare's birthday, 23 April 1993, when the
RSC was planning a celebratory service in Stratford's
Holy Trinity Church. Light relief was needed among
other more serious readings, and in searching for
something suitable, we were reminded of just how
many comic writers have used Shakespeare as raw
material for their work. Unearthing such pieces
became a hobby, until eventually the outline of a
stage show began to emerge. We had no thought of
publication until it became evident that – amazingly
in the Shakespeare Industry – nobody seemed to
have got there before us.

The backbone of this collection is a range of work
which represents the development of revue itself –
from Music Hall to Victoria Wood, via Farjeon,
Melville, Footlights and the Fringe. We hope the
other extracts from musicals, plays, comic novels and
the like, fit into a coherent whole, and we've tried to
juxtapose them in such a way as to make linking
passages superfluous. In keeping with the spirit of
revue, we have included some straight material, to
lend the programme an element of light and shade.

Of all literary and theatrical forms, revue is one of
the least documented. With no authoritative reference
book to guide us, our quest for material took us from
the manuscript collection of the British Library to a
home for retired variety performers in Twickenham,
via June Whitfield's attic. We must have overlooked
many gems along the way, and we have deliberately

omitted one or two famous names, preferring to include a proportion of lesser-known work.

Every aspect of this project – research, performance and publication – has been eased by the help we have received from a long list of friends and colleagues. First and foremost, we are conscious of the generosity of all the authors and illustrators. A full list of acknowledgements appears on page 109.

We are very grateful to Adrian Noble and everyone at the RSC, to all those who went out of their way to help us find particular pieces, and to the other members of the original cast – David Delve, Debra Gillett and Abigail McKern – who gave up precious free time to try out our various draft scripts; their commitment and expertise were invaluable in shaping the final version. We have been patiently guided through the unfamiliar world of book production by our agent Alan Brodie and our publisher Nick Hern. To all, our sincere thanks.

CHRISTOPHER LUSCOMBE AND MALCOLM MCKEE
Barbican Theatre, August 1994

Since the first edition came out last year we have completed a longer run at the Barbican, and have been able to include several brand new items by leading revue writers, bringing the scope of the show right up to date. The revue has developed under the watchful eye of Michael Codron, who is now transferring it to the West End. We are indebted to him for his constant care and attention and the wisdom he has brought to bear.

Barbican Theatre, October 1995

Note

Almost every item in *The Shakespeare Revue* has been subjected to a number of minor cuts and, very occasionally, to rewrites. This has been necessary to achieve a flow from one piece to the next, and to allow some longer extracts to fit into a revue format. For details of how to find the uncut versions, please see the acknowledgements on page 109.

The Shakespeare Revue was first performed by the Royal Shakespeare Company in The Pit on 30 October 1994. The cast comprised:

DAVID DELVE
DEBRA GILLETT
CHRISTOPHER LUSCOMBE
MALCOLM McKEE
ABIGAIL McKERN

The production was directed by Christopher Luscombe and Malcolm McKee and designed by Rob Howell, with lighting by Wayne Dowdeswell.

The revue was revived over New Year 1995 for six performances in The Pit when the cast comprised:

SUSAN BOVELL
DEBRA GILLETT
CHRISTOPHER LUSCOMBE
MALCOLM McKEE
JOHN WARNABY

It then returned to The Pit for twenty-eight perform-ances on 14 August 1995 when the cast comprised:

SUSIE BLAKE
MARTIN CONNOR
JANIE DEE
CHRISTOPHER LUSCOMBE
MALCOLM McKEE

Jenny Arnold joined the production team as choreographer.

Michael Codron transferred this production to the Vaudeville Theatre on 13 November 1995.

Part One

Prologue

If you cannot understand my argument, and declare 'It's Greek to me', you are quoting Shakespeare.

If you claim to be more sinned against than sinning, you are quoting Shakespeare.

If you recall your salad days, you are quoting Shakespeare.

If you act more in sorrow than anger, if your wish is father to the thought, if your lost property has vanished into thin air, you are quoting Shakespeare.

If you have ever refused to budge an inch, or suffered from green-eyed jealousy, if you have played fast and loose, if you have been tongue-tied, a tower of strength, hoodwinked or in a pickle, if you have knitted your brows, made a virtue of necessity, insisted on fair play or slept not one wink, had short shrift, cold comfort or too much of a good thing, if you have seen better days or lived in a fool's paradise – why, be that as it may, the more fool you, for it's a foregone conclusion that you are (as good luck would have it) quoting Shakespeare.

Even if you bid me good riddance and send me packing, if you wish I were dead as a doornail, if you think I am an eyesore, a laughing stock, the devil incarnate, a stony-hearted villain, bloody-minded or a blinking idiot, then – by Jove!

O Lord!

Tut, tut!

For goodness' sake!

What the dickens!

But me no buts!

It's all one to me,

For you are quoting Shakespeare.

Bernard Levin
From *Enthusiasms* (1983)

*Song: **The Bard of Avon***

The hottest shows on the London scene,
Honour those who have gone and been:
Piaf, Buddy, Cole Porter too –
Lives and talents shown in revue.

Gershwin, Coward, Berlin and Kern –
Song by song they have had their turn.
Side by side in the Sondheim mould,
Songs are sung and their stories told.

But the greatest of them all,
Whose works are worth the ravin',
Is the poet people call
The Bard of Stratford on Avon.

Cole Porter
From the musical *Kiss Me Kate* (1948)
Additional lyrics by **Laurence Phillips** (1995)

Who was William Shakespeare?

And so it was, at the dawning of the Elizabethan
Epoch, as it was known – that a babe was born in a
small well-known English Midlands town called
Stratford-upon-Avon (or Stratford East, Stratford
Ontario or Stratford Johns, as it was also known) –
home of Anne Hathaway's Cottage, Mary Arden's
House, Shakespeare's Birthplace and the Royal
Shakespeare Theatre Company.

And as his parents gazed down at that little new-
born Elizabethan infant, his little Elizabethan ruff
already round his little rough Elizabethan neck,
his little struggling Elizabethan body already
clad in his first little all-in-one doublet and
hose, and proudly watched him mewling
and puking all over his brand new little

Elizabethan duvet, they could not possibly have guessed what that recently sired babe – fruit of their handiwork, so to speak – *would in fact become.*

For the babe that lay before them – and already showing signs, *even as an infant,* of his famous prematurely receding forehead – was none other than that Son of Avon, the Immortal Swan himself, William Shakespeare.

In other words, the most famous man the world has ever known.

But who in fact was he?

Will we ever find out?

Or will he always remain 'shrouded in mystery'?

To answer these questions, and many more, we must now consider 'Who was William Shakespeare'?

William Geoffrey Shakespeare was born in Shakespeare's Birthplace in Stratford-upon-Avon but a stone's throw from Anne Hathaway's Cottage with whom he was to have a stormy and incestuous marriage in later years.

Unfortunately, this is all that is currently known of the extraordinary and colourful life of William Shakespeare. Which leads us, of course, to the question: *Who was William Shakespeare?*

In order to answer this we need first to ask ourselves:

Who were his parents?

Although – as we have seen – nothing whatsoever is known about his parents, we *do* know, via combing through various records and so forth, that his father was George Shakespeare or possibly even Thomas

Shakespeare, a well-known Elizabethan glove maker from Stratford's Glove Quarter (or 'Compartment', as it was also known), while his mother, of course, was Mary Arden, the popular Stratford cosmetics expert.

And finally, did Shakespeare's father's glove manufacturing influence Shakespeare's early works?

Yes, it certainly did. Shakespeare's early works are stiff with glove-manufacturing references. In fact, many whole plays were inspired by his father's obsession with constantly inventing new kinds of glove. In particular, the woollen glove which inspired *The Winter's Tale,* the animal-handling glove which inspired *The Taming of the Shrew* and, of course, the rubber glove which inspired *Pericles – Prince of Tyre.*

Patrick Barlow
From *Shakespeare: the Truth* (1993)

The Music Hall Shakespeare

Shakespeare wrote a lot of plays,
Tragedies of olden days –
Wrote 'em in a manner far from gay.
Often it occurs to me
How much brighter they would be
Written in a 'music hally' way.
Take 'To be or not to be',
Hamlet's famed soliloquy –
Nowadays the point it seems to miss;
But revise the words a bit,
Put a catchy tune to it,
And Hamlet's speech would turn out
   more like this:

CHORUS
(to the tune of *Let's all go down the Strand)*

To be, or not to be?
To be, or not to be?
If I live, Ophelia I must wed;
If I die, I'll be a long time dead.
To be, or not to be? (That is the question.)
I'm fairly up a tree.
If I die, where shall I go?
Even John Bull doesn't know.
To be, or not to be.

Take another Shakespeare play,
Very gruesome I must say,
In which Shylock plays a leading part.
He's the chap, I'm sure you know,
Who from young Antonio
Claims a pound of flesh cut near the heart.
Anger flashing from his eyes,
'Curse the Christian dog' he cries,
'I will have my pound of flesh this day.'
How much nicer it would be

If, instead of tragedy,
Shylock to Antonio did say:

CHORUS
(to the tune of *Oh! Oh! Antonio*)

'Oh! Oh! Antonio! You'll have to pay.
Though you are stoney-o
I'll get my own-y-o.
I'll have my pound of flesh
Cut from your heart,
And I'll hawk it round at fourpence a pound
On my ice-cream cart.'

Next a character I'll quote,
From a play that Shakespeare wrote –
King Henry VIII – a wicked lot!
Half a dozen wives had he,
'Cos when with one he couldn't agree,
He divorced her, and a fresh one got.
Till at last, in righteous wrath,
Wolsey cried out 'By my troth,
This man's a libertine – off with his head!'
But if that had been a play
On the music halls today,
Wolsey would have simply winked and said:

CHORUS
(to the tune of *It's a Different Girl Again*)

'Hello! Hello! Hello! It's a different wife again;
With different eyes, different nose,
Different hair, different clothes.
Hello! Hello! Hello! To me it's fairly plain
He's tickled the chin of Anne Boleyn,
It's a different wife again.'

Words by **Worton David**
Music by **Harry Fragson** (*c.*1905)

I'm in the RSC!

April 1977:
I'm in the RSC!
I'm in the RSC!
This is the right place, the best place for me!
To look out at that audience, to stand here on this
    stage!
Possibly-the-greatest-Shakespearean-actor-perhaps-
    of-this-age!
Part of the best work the British Theatre's ever done,
And I'll say that the moment I meet Trevor Nunn.

I'm in the RSC!
(Or should it be *I'm* in the RSC?
Or I'm in the R*SC*?)
Anyway, it's just amazing that *they* pay *me*!
I've got a tiny part in
The thing with John Barton;
I'm just a fairy
For Terry,
But then I am just startin'.
The main thing is hard work and keenness and
    endeavour.
I'm bound to be noticed before long by Trevor.

But O! For shame! *Disillusioned* I feel!
Now starts my head from confusion to reel.
Methinks I consented, aye, foolishly fast,
Signing a contract to play just 'as cast'.
I stand mute on battlements, mounds, rocks
    and carts,
Now understudy I seventeen parts.
Henceforth to have my voice heard I'll persever;

I'll SSSSENNND FOR A PARLEYYYYY!!!
I wanna see Trevor.

I've been covered in mud, I've shrieked up the aisle
For Bogdanov and Davies and Daniels and Kyle;
I've faffed with Francesca, ha-ha-ha'd around Helen,
Been gobbed on by Pennington, Sinden, McKellen.
I'm tired of being A Roman, A Trojan, A Greek;
Tired of yelping and moaning – I JUST WANT TO
    SPEAK!
I watch them cock it up through scenes everlasting –
I just don't understand their ideas about casting.

ROMEO & JULIET
MARIE KEAN as Nurse
FRANCESCA ANNIS as Juliet
IAN McKELLEN as Romeo
MICHAEL PENNINGTON as Mercutio

How could that gnome
Be the noblest in Rome?
Why has that pisser
Been given Nerissa?
I know you get bums on seats when you cast a star,
But this time I really think they've gone too far.
I mean, offering Frank Bruno Aaron the Moor;
I'm sure he'd do Stratford, but would he tour?

Nightly crippling my body and gunging my face,
Whooh! things'd be different if I ran this place.
We're the best, but face it, here's the rub,
Is there *enough* anguished, intense bitching going
    on in the pub?
And OK, so SUDDENLY they're offering me Prince
    Hal, Timon, Autolycus and Richard Three –
Well, too bad, they can stick it, they've done
    NOTHING for me.
And I'll bring all this up if I get to see EVER
That elusive, fffly-by-night, absentee – TREVOR!!!
How ARE you? They all say that *Sunset Boulevard*'s
    brilliantly clever . . .

Jack Klaff (1981)

Song:

If You Go Down to the Vault Tonight

If you go down to the vault tonight, you're sure of
    a big surprise;
If you go down to the vault tonight, it mightn't be
    very wise;
        But if you dare, you'd better take care:
        There's Montague blood on the bill of fare –
Tonight's the night the Capulets have their picnic.

If you go down to the vault tonight on one of your
    graveyard trips,
You'll find a genuine corpse all right – poor Juliet's
    had her chips.
        She lay so fair in her bridal wear,
        And woke to stare at Romeo there –
Enough to put the Capulets off their picnic.

Words by **Mary Holtby** (1985)
Music by **John W. Bratton** (1947)

And How Is Hamlet?

Elsinore. A platform before the castle. From one side of the stage the AMBASSADOR *enters. From the other, four* GENTLEMEN *of the court who, on seeing the* AMBASSADOR, *rush to grasp his hand in hearty greeting.*

FIRST GENT: Welcome my worthy lord, at last returned
From foreign lands, thy mission done and blest
With fortune's fruitage and the palms of peace.

SECOND GENT: All Elsinore this greeting gives to thee
With one unstinting universal tongue.

AMBASSADOR: I thank thee, sirs. Full welcome do I feel
After my three years absence. I have been
Ambassador too long in lands remote
In loyal service to the Danish crown;
And here before the castle's ramparts high
My heart doth leap, like to the roistering vole
In native glades delighting. (*Eagerly*) Gentlemen,
Tell me, I pray, how goes the Danish state?
What toys, what changes, fashions, shifts and turns?
(*With deep affection*) And how is Hamlet, Denmark's
    dear delight?
Young Hamlet, witty, jocund, kind and free,
Of liberal heart and manner nobly sweet,
Poetic Hamlet, hope of all the land,
Life of our life and loadstar of our fate,
Dancer, mimic, soldier, raconteur,
Philosopher and favourite of the gods.

FIRST GENT: (*with difficulty*) Hamlet, my lord . . . is
    dead.

    Pause.

AMBASSADOR: (*shocked*) What? Hamlet dead?

16

Alas! but how came Hamlet thus to die?

SECOND GENT: Young Hamlet died in duelling, gentle
    sir.
He fought the young Laertes, also dead.

AMBASSADOR: (*appalled*) Laertes dead?

THIRD GENT: A corpse who even now
Is freshly festering in a nearby grave
With all the zest of youth.

AMBASSADOR: How did he die?

FIRST GENT: In combat keen against our former
    Prince
For vengeance of his sister, lately mad.

AMBASSADOR: The fair Ophelia?

FOURTH GENT: *Foul* Ophelia, sir.
For she lies decomposing, though her wits
Rotted before her.

SECOND GENT: 'Twas her father's death.

AMBASSADOR: (*distressed*) The fair Polonius?

THIRD GENT: Dead, sir, dead as well.
Slain by Prince Hamlet who, as you have heard,
Is also dead.

AMBASSADOR: How tragic for the Queen.

FIRST GENT: Gertrude, I fear, has passed beyond such
    pain,
Plucked off by poison, from the King's own hand.

AMBASSADOR: Is't possible? King Claudius, he who
    reigns?

FIRST GENT: Who *reigned*, my friend, for he is quite
    reigned out.
Young Hamlet too hath heaved him up to Heaven.

AMBASSADOR: And Hamlet's father?

THIRD GENT: Deader than the rest:
He died before the killing had begun.
He's now a ghost and often can be heard
Intoning on these very battlements.

AMBASSADOR: (*becoming desperate*) And Osric, the
  effeminate courtier?

SECOND GENT: Dead of exertion following the duel.

  AMBASSADOR *groans in general grief.*

SECOND GENT: A hideous scene of blood and, as I fear,
A heavy sight to greet young Fortinbras.

AMBASSADOR: Young Fortinbras?

FOURTH GENT: The conquering prince who came,
Moonlike, to view the slaughter of the field,
Pale monarch of the slumbering citadel –
Inheritor of Denmark's empty crown.

  Pause.

AMBASSADOR: So Fortinbras is King in Denmark now.
How is he?

SECOND GENT: He is dead, my lord, as well.

AMBASSADOR: How came he too to die? It seems most
  strange.

SECOND GENT: Struck dead by all the news of all the
  dead.
The fatal tidings shocked his delicate spirit
And called it to repose.

  AMBASSADOR *sighs heavily.*

THIRD GENT: He died soon after
He heard the bloody summary from the lips
Of Horatio.

FOURTH GENT: The late Horatio.

AMBASSADOR: Alas Horatio! And is he gone as well?

18

FIRST GENT: Gone, gone, my lord, to dally in the dust.
No sooner had he voiced his bitter tale
Than, taking out the sword he ever kept
For just such moments, plunged it with a sigh
Into the scabbard of his heaving heart
And, shortly, slept.

AMBASSADOR: (*greatly moved*) O grievous anecdote.

SECOND GENT: And others too hath ta'en their loyal
lives
With swords and bodkins, cannons, spears and
knives:
Marcellus and Bernardo and a Priest . . .

THIRD GENT: Reynaldo and Francisco and the
Players . . .

FOURTH GENT: A Gentleman, a Captain and two
Clowns.

FIRST GENT: The 'Dramatis Personae', as it were.

AMBASSADOR: (*with a sense of discovery*) So Death,
I see, doth suit the tragic scene;
To be is not to be, but to have been.

The AMBASSADOR *unsheathes his sword.*

(*Bravely*) Come, valiant friends, we needs must
wander towards
Some nether room, and fall upon our swords.

The others agree manfully, and they and the
AMBASSADOR *exit.*

Perry Pontac
From *Hamlet, Part II* (1992)

Song: *Moody Dane*

Moody Dane,
Moody Dane,
Why are
You moody?
Broody Dane,
Broody Dane,
Don't be
So broody!
Smile a smile, dear,
Dry your eyes,
Try not to
Soliloquize.
Don't keep sayin':
'That's the question,'
It is only
Indigestion –

Moody Dane,
Moody Dane,
Don't be
So naughty!
It is all
Wrong to call
Your Momma
Bawdy –
There's a bend in every lane,
Soon the sun will shine again,
Skies of blue come after rain,
Moody Dane,
Moody Dane.

Words by **Herbert Farjeon**
Music by **John Pritchett**
From the revue *Nine Sharp* (1938)

Song: *Give Us A Rest*

Trio for HAMLET, JULIET *and* HENRY V

ALL: We don't need an introduction
    – more's the pity!
We're afraid we're quite familiar
    to you all.
Our time-honoured conversation's
Simply bursting with quotations
Which you poor things had to
    learn when you were small.
We're appearing here tonight
    to make it cle-ar
That though you may be tired of us
You can't be half as tired as we are.

Give us a rest, we implore you.
Give us a rest is all our plea.
We're fed up with being acted
And we'd like to be subtracted
From the repertoire of ev'ry company.
We feel we've done our duty by the public
And we know we've always given of our best,

JULIET: But Romeo and I would love to get to know
    our grave.

HENRY V: And both my arms are aching from this
    sword I have to wave.

HAMLET: And I've begun to realise why I'm called a
    peasant slave.

ALL: Give us a rest, give us a rest, give us a rest.

HAMLET: I'm encored
But I'm bored,
And I'm retiring to the closet indisposed.

JULIET: I am sick
Of the Vic,
And I've a notice on my balcony which says 'We
    never closed'.

HENRY V: I'm so madly patriotic
That it's making me neurotic,
And I'm sick of climbing through that ruddy breech.

ALL: We've been done upon the stage, on the radio
    and the screen.

JULIET: I've been done by girls of forty when I'm
    s'posed to be fourteen.

ALL: We've been done in sev'ral periods which we
    found extremely weird.

HAMLET: I've been done by Alec Guinness in a rather
    nasty beard.

ALL: Peter Brook and Tyrone Guthrie, Donald Wolfit
    and the lot
Have used us to express we're never sure exactly
    what,
And if none of us rebels
We'll be done by Orson Welles,
So please forgive us, if we beseech –

Give us a rest – are you list'ning?
Give us a rest – or shoot us dead!
And for heaven's sake protect us
From those Amazon directors,
Let them loose on *Lear* or *Pericles* instead.

HAMLET AND HENRY V: We've both of us been done by
   Mr Branagh,

HAMLET: And once was quite enough, I would
   suggest.

JULIET: We're going to make a stand, no matter what it
   may involve.

HAMLET: And in the last resort to go on strike is our
   resolve –

HENRY V: Before young Daldry puts us on the
   National's revolve –

Juliet screams.

ALL: Give us a rest!
Give us a rest!
Give us a rest!

Sandy Wilson
From the revue *See You Later* (1953)
Additional lyrics (1994)

The Man Who Speaks in Anagrams

PALIN: Our next guest is a man who speaks entirely in anagrams.

IDLE: Taht si crreoct.

PALIN: Do you enjoy it?

IDLE: I stom certainly od. Revy chum so.

PALIN: And what's your name?

IDLE: Hamrag – Hamrag Yatlerot.

PALIN: Well, Graham, nice to have you on the show. Now, where do you come from?

IDLE: Bumcreland.

PALIN: Cumberland?

IDLE: Staht sit sepricly.

PALIN: And I believe you're working on an anagram version of Shakespeare?

IDLE: Sey, sey - taht si crreoct, er – ta the mnemot I'm wroking on *The Mating of the Wersh*.

PALIN: The *Mating of the Wersh*? By William Shakespeare?

IDLE: Nay, by Malliwi Rapesheake.

PALIN: And what else?

IDLE: *Two Netlemeg of Verona*, *Twelfth Thing*, *The Chamrent of Venice* . . .

PALIN: Have you done *Hamlet*?

IDLE: *Thamle*. 'Be ot or bot ne ot, tath is the nestqui.'

PALIN: And what is your next project?

IDLE: *Ring Kichard the Thrid.*

PALIN: I'm sorry?

IDLE: 'A shroe! A shroe! My dingkome for a shroe!'

PALIN: Ah, Ring Kichard, yes but surely that's not an anagram, that's a spoonerism.

IDLE: If you're going to split hairs I'm going to piss off.

From *Monty Python's Flying Circus* (1972)

Overlooked by Alan Howard, Michael Gambon does his Olivier impression.

Shakespeare Masterclass

DIRECTOR: All right, let's start at the beginning shall we?

ACTOR: Right, yeh.

DIRECTOR: What's the word, what's the word, I wonder, that Shakespeare decides to begin his sentence with here?

ACTOR: Er, 'Time' is the first word.

DIRECTOR: Time, Time.

ACTOR: Yep.

DIRECTOR: And how does Shakespeare decide to spell it, Hugh?

ACTOR: T-I-M-E.

DIRECTOR: T-I?

ACTOR: M.

DIRECTOR: M-E.

ACTOR: Yep.

DIRECTOR: And what sort of spelling of the word is that?

ACTOR: Well it's the ordinary spelling.

DIRECTOR: It's the *ordinary* spelling, isn't it? It's the *conventional* spelling. So why out of all the spellings he could have chosen, did Shakespeare choose that one, do you think?

ACTOR: Well, um, because it gives us time in an ordinary sense.

DIRECTOR: Exactly, well done, good boy. Because it gives us time in an ordinary, conventional sense.

ACTOR: Oh, right.

DIRECTOR: So, Shakespeare has given us time in a conventional sense. But he's given us something else, Hugh. Have a look at the typography. What do you spy?

ACTOR: Oh, it's got a capital T.

DIRECTOR: Shakespeare's T is very much upper case, there, Hugh, isn't it? Why?

ACTOR: 'Cos it's the first word in the sentence.

DIRECTOR: Well I think that's *partly* it. But I think there's another reason too. Shakespeare has given us time in a *conventional* sense – and time in an *abstract* sense.

ACTOR: Right, yes.

DIRECTOR: All right? Think your voice can convey that, Hugh?

ACTOR: I hope so.

DIRECTOR: I hope so too. All right. Give it a go.

ACTOR: Just the one word?

DIRECTOR: Just the one word for the moment.

ACTOR: Yep. (*He howls the word*) TIME!

DIRECTOR: Wo, wo, wo. Where do we gather from?

ACTOR: Oh, the buttocks.

DIRECTOR: Always the buttocks. Gather from the buttocks. Thank you.

ACTOR: (*gathering*) Time!

DIRECTOR: Well, there are a number of things I liked about that, Hugh, there was . . . there was . . . there was a number of things I liked about that. All right, try it again, and this time try and bring in a sense of Troy falling, a sense of ruin, of folly, of anger, of decay, of hopelessness and despair, a sense of greed –

ACTOR: Ambition?

DIRECTOR: No, leave ambition out for the moment if you would, Hugh, of greed, of mortality, and of transience. All right? And try to suffuse the whole thing with a red colour . . .

ACTOR: Time!

DIRECTOR: What went wrong there, Hugh?

ACTOR: I don't know. I got a bit lost in the middle actually.

Stephen Fry and **Hugh Laurie**
From the revue *The Cellar Tapes* (1981)

Song:
The Heroine the Opera House Forgot

When Shakespeare wrote a plot, he
Never could have known,
That one day Pavarotti
Would make the plays his own.
Otello, he has dropped his 'h' to take his opera bow,
The Merry Wives of Windsor are scheming divas now;
And, by the way, The Scottish Play has arias by the
    mile.
But even Verdi could not score with the Siren of the
    Nile.

(*La Donna è Mobile pastiche*)

CHORUS: Poor Cleopatera
Opera won't flatter her,
After all she'd a
Been as good as Aida.
Falstaff and Whatsisname,
Scotsman in Dunsinane –
Not quite heady as
Cleo by Verdi
Cleo . . . Cleo by Verdi.

(*Caro Nome pastiche*)

CLEOPATRA: As they laid me to my rest,
With a serpent at my breast,
Immortality in store
Through the Bard and Bernard Shaw.
Hollywood would treat me good, and a Carry On
    on the telly;

Where I'd indulge Sid James's whim,
In a bath of semi-skim,
But I'd rather be played yet
At the Garden or the Met.

CHORUS: She's the heroine the opera house forgot,
CLEOPATRA: In the quartos and the folios I rot.
CHORUS: Maestro Verdi why such Malice?
CLEOPATRA: I was never sung by Callas!
I'm the heroine the opera house forgot.

(*Traviata pastiche*)

CHORUS: Lovely plots
Feature lots
Of young scots
One might slay,
Or a spot that will not go away;
Or there's more
Than a Moor
Who is for
Amore,
'Til outflanked by a hanky one day.

CLEOPATRA: I beseech you Signor Verdi,
For my aria I am ready,
My vivacious viva voce
Has vigour, verve and valliance;
Oh Giuseppe, I am Peppy,
With a penchant for Italians –
The show will not be over
'Til the asp lady sings.

CHORUS: And bingo how she'd sing – oh
For a ding-dong with Domingo.

She'd be cheery done by Kiri –
Lots of trills and thrills and clarity.
She'd be pert and rather flirty
If portrayed by Lesley Garretty.
Sarah Brightman as this Diva
In the right man sparks a fever.

CLEOPATRA: Surely opera is the poorer
Without Cleopatra colloratura!

CHORUS: Brava Cleopatra, brava Cleo,
Brava Cleo,
Brava Cleopatra,
Brava!

Words by **Laurence Phillips**
Music by **Carlton Edwards** /
Joe Green
(Arr. **Carlton Edwards**) (1995)

Swap a Jest

FIRST CLOWN: I say, I say, I say! Well met i'faith.

SECOND CLOWN: Well met indeed. But whence cometh?

FIRST CLOWN: I cometh from the house of Mistress Quickly.

SECOND CLOWN: Mistress Quickly, Mistress Quickly. She is somewhat of a fast one.

FIRST CLOWN: Think on't, think on't. 'Tis in jest. Nay, nay, verily, forsooth, I've been having trouble with the Black Death.

SECOND CLOWN: Wilt thou keep my mother-in-law out of this.

FIRST CLOWN: Tarry for it, better cometh. My spouse, my spouse, she's been unfaithful.

SECOND CLOWN: Does she play the strumpet?

FIRST CLOWN: Yes, and she's no virginal either.

SECOND CLOWN: I don't wish to know that, kindly leave the Globe.

FIRST CLOWN: Shall I tell thee a topical tale?

SECOND CLOWN: Do tell, do tell.

FIRST CLOWN: Her Majesty the Queen . . .

SECOND CLOWN: God bless her, God bless her.

FIRST CLOWN: . . . was descending from a coach the other day into a puddle.

SECOND CLOWN: Into a puddle right up to her . . . ? – No.

FIRST CLOWN: No. And she said to Sir Walter Raleigh . . .

SECOND CLOWN: What did she say, what did she say?

FIRST CLOWN: Where are the cloaks?

SECOND CLOWN: And he replied . . .

33

FIRST CLOWN: First right and follow the rush matting.

SECOND CLOWN: Are you sure 'twas he?

FIRST CLOWN: Yes, 'twas Sir Walter, Raleigh.

SECOND CLOWN: Shall we finish with a song?

FIRST CLOWN: Yes, a lute song. A really lute song.
Minstrel, prithee . . .

BOTH: (*sung*)
When the wheel of fortune runs you down,
And the heavens above are grey,
Just step a measure,
Swap a jest
And sing a roundelay.
Remember all the world's a stage,
That's what the poets said,
So step a measure,
Swap a jest
And sing a roundelay.
Hey nonny!
Sing a roundelay.
It swingeth!
Sing a roundelay!

Tim Brooke-Taylor and **Bill Oddie**
From the revue *Cambridge Circus* (1963)

Song: *Which Witch?*

It is many a year since I launched my career in
    Shakespeare.
At a most tender age I first tottered on stage as a page.
I was with Johnnie G. in – now when would it be?
    Forty-three.
Larry *was* such a dear, so I carried a spear in his *Lear*.

Ah! Those were the days, I'm sure you'll agree,
But last week a fringe group from Clacton-on-Sea
Asked me to tour (it's non-Equity rules;
You sleep in the van, and play prisons and schools),
For eighty-nine weeks as a witch in Macbeth –
A prospect, I thought, little better than death.
But as I'd grown tired of just giving auditions,
I said I would do it, on certain conditions.

I told the director, 'My dear,
There is one point on which I'm not clear.
We've fixed up the sordid finance, so to speak,
And I'm working for practic'lly nothing a week,
But in which part am I to appear?

MACBETH: "FILTHY HAGS! WHY DO YOU SHOW ME THIS? – A FOURTH? – START, EYES! – WHAT WILL
THE LINE STRETCH OUT TO TH' CRACK OF DOOM? – ANOTHER YET..."

'Which witch?
Is it First Witch, or Second, or which?
As one who's played Lady Macbeth in her day,
I must be the witch with the most lines to say.
The tall, scraggy thin one does not int'rest me:
I must be the hag with the gag in Act Three.
If it's the First Witch, my dear, I should love it;
But if it's the Second, you know where you can
    shove it.
The Second Witch part is of slender repute:
(Though it's got *one* good line – can't *I* say 'eye of
    newt'?)
To avoid any last-minute hitch,
Would you kindly inform me which witch?

'Yes, before I pack one single bag,
I must know in advance, dear, which hag?
There's only one crone, dear, which frankly will do,
And I don't mean Crone Three, and I *don't* mean
    Crone Two.
It would save some expense if you didn't have
    three:
Why not lump them together, and only have me?
D'you know, dear, I think it would work
If *I* were to say 'nose of Turk',
And that bit about drabs in a ditch –
I just want to know, dear, *which* raddled old crow,
    dear – which witch?

'And another thing, dear, would you care
To explain what the witches will wear?'
    He said 'Nothing, they're nude, not a stitch . . . '
    – so I never discovered which witch.

Words by **Alan Melville**
Music by **Charles Zwar**
From the revue *Sky High* (1942)
Additional lyrics by **Jeremy Browne** (1995)

Song: *Away with the Fairies*

PEASEBLOSSOM: Ready!

MOTH: And I!

COBWEB: And I!

MUSTARDSEED: And I!

FIRST FAIRY: And I!

PEASEBLOSSOM: Ready!

MOTH: And I!

COBWEB: And I!

MUSTARDSEED: And I!

FIRST FAIRY: And I!

ALL: Yes, but what are we ready for?
    What are we ready for?
    What studied torments hast thou in store for us,
    Herr Direktor? Herr Direktor?

PEASEBLOSSOM: Ready!

MOTH: And I!

COBWEB: And I!

MUSTARDSEED: And I!

FIRST FAIRY: And I!

PEASEBLOSSOM: Peaseblossom!

MOTH: Moth!

COBWEB: Cobweb!

MUSTARDSEED: Mustardseed!

FIRST FAIRY: A Fairy!

ALL: Yes, we're fairies!
    You wouldn't know it to look at us;

FIRST FAIRY: I blame the director;

ALL: We all do;

FIRST FAIRY: We have rolled around in mud and we
    have swung on a trapeze;

ALL: Ah! Ah!

FIRST FAIRY: We have studied Polish mime and we
    have imitated bees;

ALL: Ah! Ah!

FIRST FAIRY: But we hate it;
    How we hate it!
    How we wish we had wings!
    How we wish we had wings!

ALL: For when we had wings, we would float like
        thistledown;
    Hang pearls in a cowslip's ear;
    And swing on the air;
    As light as the breeze, all attired in gossamer;
    Ah then we would fly away.

Dillie Keane (1995)

Song: *Fear No More*

(*Spoken*) No exorciser harm thee!
Nor no witchcraft charm thee!
Ghost unlaid forbear thee!
Nothing ill come near thee!
Quiet consummation have,
And renowned be thy grave!

(*Sung*) Fear no more the heat o' th' sun
Nor the furious winter's rages;
Thou thy worldy task has done,
Home art gone, and ta'en thy wages:
Golden lads and girls all must,
As chimney sweepers, come to dust.

Fear no more the lightning-flash,
Nor th'all-dreaded thunder-stone;
Fear not slander, censure rash;
Thou hast finish'd joy and moan:
All lovers young, all lovers must
Consign to thee and come to dust.

Words by **William Shakespeare**
Music by **Stephen Sondheim**
From the musical *The Frogs* (1974)

Othello in Earnest

LADY BRABANTIO *and* OTHELLO, *just after tea. They speak in the distinctive accents of, respectively, Lady Bracknell and John Worthing.*

LADY BRABANTIO: Excellent cucumber sandwiches, Mr Othello.

OTHELLO: I'm so pleased you enjoyed them, Lady Brabantio.

LADY BRABANTIO: And now, to our business. You wish to marry my daughter, Desdemona, I believe.

OTHELLO: Yes, Lady Brabantio, very much so.

LADY BRABANTIO: I see. In that case I have a few questions to put to you. (*She takes out her notebook and pencil.*) What is the source of your income?

OTHELLO: I am a soldier, Lady Brabantio – from an old military family.

LADY BRABANTIO: (*taking notes*) Ah.

OTHELLO: I am, I'm afraid, often out of Venice: slaughtering the infidel, sacking and burning towns, beheading prisoners.

LADY BRABANTIO: I am pleased to hear it. A man who remains at home can do incalculable harm. My husband Lord Brabantio is a case in point. The more domestic he becomes, the more savage his behaviour seems to be. And now, your property.

OTHELLO: Two main residences, Lady Brabantio. A bachelor flat near the Bridge of Sighs and a large Gothic mansion on the Rialto.

LADY BRABANTIO: That is most satisfactory. And were you born in one of the great houses on the Canal, or did you rise from the rural simplicity of a country seat?

OTHELLO: (*reluctantly*) I'm afraid I was born . . . elsewhere, Lady Brabantio.

LADY BRABANTIO: (*surprised*) Elsewhere, Mr Othello?

OTHELLO: Yes. (*Evasively*) Rather far away, in fact.

LADY BRABANTIO: (*disapprovingly*) Far away? And where, precisely, 'far away' were you born?

OTHELLO: In . . . in Africa, Lady Brabantio.

LADY BRABANTIO: (*Lady Bracknell-like*) Africa?

OTHELLO: Yes. In a tiny village in Africa. Kajabufu. I was born in a small military fortification as it happens, a simple hut made of mud and dung; my nappy a banana-leaf, my rattle a quiver of poisoned arrows, my cradle a sandbag.

LADY BRABANTIO: (*even more Lady Bracknell-like*) A sandbag?

OTHELLO: Yes, Lady Brabantio. There in a clearing in the great jungle where the she-elephant suckles her young.

LADY BRABANTIO: (*on a rising note of disapproval*) And how, if I may ask, did you come to be raised on a sandbag in a hut in a clearing where the she-elephant suckles her young? It seems most improbable.

OTHELLO: My parents were Africans, Lady Brabantio – as am I.

LADY BRABANTIO: (*appalled*) Indeed? Not blackamoors?

OTHELLO: Quite. Father was a warrior-chief, Mother his favourite wife. (*Shakespeareanly*) Haply, for I am black . . .

LADY BRABANTIO: Not happily at all, Mr Othello. I had assumed, from your appearance, that you had recently been basking in the sun at one of our well-known seaside resorts. Indeed, this puts, if I may say so, an entirely new complexion on the matter. Yet, let us continue. I have almost completed my questions and I always finish what I begin, especially if there is no reason to do so. That is the meaning of thoroughness.

She takes up her pencil.

Now, your education. Which of our great universities did you attend?

OTHELLO: None I'm afraid. No formal education at all. My childhood was spent climbing the banyan tree, sporting naked in the sunshine, foraging for nuts and grubs with 'Maputu' the wart-hog.

LADY BRABANTIO: (*not impressed*) I see. And as an adult?

OTHELLO: As a soldier I have had many remarkable adventures which Desdemona, dear girl, has often begged me to recount. I have known disasters as well: sold into slavery, shipwrecked on the Isle of Wight for several weeks, and I have been scalped – on two different occasions – by the dreaded Norijwanee tribe of Sumatra.

LADY BRABANTIO: To be scalped once, Mr Othello, may be regarded as a misfortune; to be scalped twice looks like hairlessness.

OTHELLO: (*continuing his story, trying to impress her*) In Kashina I was nearly eaten by a lion who sprang upon me in the most unexpected manner.

Lady Brabantio remains unmoved.

It was a fierce Nemean lion, Lady Brabantio.

LADY BRABANTIO: The lion is immaterial. Mr Othello, I confess your history has filled me with disquiet.

A life such as yours, with a person such as yourself, is hardly the destiny I have in mind for Desdemona.

OTHELLO: But what is it you advise me to do? I adore the divine Desdemona.

LADY BRABANTIO: I advise you to quit your suit and to avoid my daughter forever. Desdemona has a noble nature and will be certain to forget you almost instantly.

OTHELLO: I see. Ah, the pity of it, if I may say so Lady Brabantio, the pity of it.

LADY BRABANTIO: Mr Othello, you seem, if I'm not mistaken, to be displaying signs of considerable self-esteem.

OTHELLO: (*sadly*) On the contrary, Lady Brabantio, I've now realised for the first time in my life the vital importance of being burnished.

They freeze in tableau. Black-out.

Perry Pontac (1995)

"LOOK TO YOUR WIFE; OBSERVE HER WELL WITH CASSIO." (*OTHELLO*)

Song: *Carrying a Torch*

When I was a schoolgirl
I went to see *Macbeth*,
But Shakespeare to that schoolgirl
Was the kiss of death;
And I vowed I'd never see another play,
Until that day
On the Underground,
I still recall,
On the Underground
That poster on the wall.

I saw his face,
Strong yet sweet,
Phoned this place,
Booked a seat.

And any moment now
I'll be seeing him once more,
This is my third visit in a week.
Any moment now
He'll be coming through that door,
And this is where we get to hear him speak.
He wears the sort of toga
That Roman servants would,
Bringing lines to life I never understood.
Though it's not at all
What the critics call
A glittering career,
I'm still carrying a torch for the boy
Who's carrying a spear.

Any moment now
It will be the Ides of March,

He's in the wings just waiting to appear.
Any moment now
He will walk beneath that arch,
With news that Caesar doesn't want to hear.
All throughout the season
I've watched him on that stage,
One night as a soldier, next night as a page.
And although he may
Never get to play
King Richard or King Lear,
I'm still carrying a torch for the boy
Who's carrying a spear.

Any moment now,
Any moment now . . .

(*Spoken*) 'They would not have you stir forth today.
Plucking the entrails of an offering forth,
They could not find a heart within the beast.'

Any moment now
In the first scene of Act Three,
He has to grieve when Caesar is deceased.
Any moment now,
It's so wonderful to see,
I have found a heart within the beast.
For as that silly schoolgirl
It seems that I was blind;
He gave me the key that's opened up my mind.
And although as yet
We have never met,
I hope the day draws near,
For I'm carrying a torch for the boy
Who's carrying a spear.

Words by **Anthony Drewe**
Music by **George Stiles** (1995)

Giving Notes

Right. Bit of hush please. Connie! Thank you. Now
that was quite a good rehearsal; I was quite pleased.
There were a few raised eyebrows when we let it
slip the Piecrust Players were having a bash at
Shakespeare but I think we're getting there. But I
can't say this too often: it may be *Hamlet* but it's got
to be Fun Fun Fun!

Now we're still very loose on lines. Where's Gertrude?
I'm not so worried about you – if you 'dry' just give
us a bit of business with the shower cap. But Barbara
– you will have to buckle down. I mean, Ophelia's
mad scene, 'There's rosemary, that's for remem-
brance' – it's no good just bunging a few herbs about
and saying, 'Don't mind me, I'm a loony'. Yes?

Right, Act One Scene One, on the ramparts. Now I
know the whist table is a bit wobbly, but until Stan
works out how to adapt the Beanstalk it'll have to
do. What's this? Atmosphere? Yes – now what did
we work on, Philip? Yes, it's midnight, it's jolly cold.
What do we do when it's cold? We go 'Brrr', and we
do this *(slaps hands on arms)*. Right, well don't forget
again, please. And cut the hot-water bottle, it's not
working.

Where's my ghost of Hamlet's father? Oh yes, what
went wrong tonight, Betty? He's on nights still, is he?
OK. Well, it's not really on for you to play that
particular part, Betty – you're already doing the
Player Queen and the back legs of Hamlet's donkey.
Well, we don't know he didn't have one, do we?
Why waste a good cossy?

Hamlet – drop the Geordie, David, it's not coming over. Your characterisation's reasonably good, David, but it's just far too gloomy. Fair enough, make him a little bit depressed at the beginning, but start lightening it from Scene Two, say from the hokey-cokey onwards.

Polonius, try and show the age of the man in your voice and in your bearing, rather than waving the bus-pass. I think you'll find it easier when we get the walking frame. Is that coming, Connie? OK.

The Players' scene: did any of you feel it had stretched a bit too . . . ? Yes. I think we'll go back to the tumbling on the entrance, rather than the extract from *Barnum.* You see, we're running at six hours twenty now, and if we're going to put those soliloquies back in . . .

Gravediggers? Oh yes, gravediggers. The problem here is that Shakespeare hasn't given us a lot to play with – I feel we're a little short on laughs, so Harold, you do your dribbling, and Arthur, just put in anything you can remember from the Ayckbourn, yes?

The mad scene: apart from lines, much better, Barbara – I can tell you're getting more used to the straitjacket. Oh – any news on the skull, Connie? I'm just thinking, if your little dog pulls through, we'll have to fall back on papier mâché. All right, Connie, as long as it's dead by the dress . . .

That's it for tonight then; thank you. I shall expect you all to be word-perfect by the next rehearsal. Have any of you realised what date we're up to? Yes, April the twenty-seventh! And when do we open? August! It's not long!

Victoria Wood
From *Up to You, Porky* (1985)

Song: *In Shakespeare's Day*

WARDROBE MISTRESS: Another bloody doublet,
Another flaming ruff.
We're connoisseurs of Shakespeare
Though we can't stand the stuff.
Still, working in the wardrobe
Is fun in fits and starts,
We get to meet the actors;
We get to know their parts.
Another new designer with problems we must fix,
But hessian and sackcloth
Is murder on me quicks.
The thing that's most amazing
Is not the ruddy play,
It's how they managed without velcro
In Shakespeare's day.

ICE-CREAM SELLER: Another flavoured ice cream,
A new exotic tub.
Forget about the play, dear,
But come and buy the grub.
Vanilla or stem ginger,
They'll set you back a quid;
White chocolate or strawberry,
The spoon's inside the lid.
Does anyone need programmes
Stuffed full with 'thees' and 'thous'?
I've heard it said that Shakespeare
Was just a big girl's blouse.
But what is more intriguing
Than knowing if he's gay,
Is how they managed without freezers
In Shakespeare's day.

PROMPT: Another trendy version,
The same old boring cast.
I prompt them from the wings,
'Course my repertoire is vast.
I'm not big on directors
Who choose to change the text,
For 'new interpretation'
Read 'Christ, what happens next?'
Another set of changes, another load of guff,
Four hundred years of rewrites
You'd think would be enough.
They say it's good to question,
My question, if I may,
Is how they managed without Tippex
In Shakespeare's day.

MUSICIAN: Another major fanfare,
Another minor chord.
There's not a flipping gesture
That isn't underscored.
I have to play the music
To which the kings can flounce,
Dreamt up by that composer
Whose name I can't pronounce.
My favourite work of Shakespeare's
A musical of his,
The one with those French soldiers –
You must have seen *Les Miz*,
But what I often wonder
Is how they used to play
Without a single synthesizer
In Shakespeare's day.

PROPS: Another court to furnish,
Another list of props.
They're not the sort of items
You find in high street shops.
A clack-dish and a bird-bolt
Two gorgets and a tuck,
I think that Mr. Noble
Should take a flying visit around a few junk shops
    and see if he can find some of the ridiculous
    things he expects me to dig up.
Another moody monarch, another bleedin' throne,
You'd think they'd be recycled
No . . . each one has his own.
I'd best go have a rummage
It's gonna turn me grey,
How did they cope without car boot sales
In Shakespeare's Day . . .

ALL: . . . and night
His every verse and sonnet

50

Keeps us all in work,
And we depend upon it.
Odd to think
The man wrote with a feather,
Yet his ink
Has brought us all together.

WARDROBE MISTRESS: With another padded codpiece –

ICE-CREAM SELLER: Another new cornetto –

PROMPT: Another flashing cue light –

MUSICIAN: Another bunch of crotchets –

PROPS: Some loggats and a bombard –

WARDROBE. Another set of garters –

ICE-CREAM SELLER: The spoon's inside the lid –

PROMPT: Another load of changes –

ICE-CREAM SELLER: The spoon's inside the lid –

MUSICIAN: Involuntary trumpets –

ICE-CREAM SELLER: The spoon's inside the lid! –

PROPS: A budget full of groats –

ICE-CREAM SELLER: THE SPOON'S INSIDE THE LID!

ALL: Another new production
The critics say 'It's brave';
But hark! That must be Shakespeare
Spinning in his grave.
No doubt he's just as puzzled
To understand the way
In which they managed without us
In Shakespeare's day.

Words by **Anthony Drewe**
Music by **George Stiles** (1995)

Part Two

The troublesome reign of Ricardinia II

Hewison / The Times

Song: *PC or not PC*

English plays through the dance of time,
From comedy and tragedy to pantomime,
From curtain up to tender ending,
Have more than a touch of gender bending.

Thus Rosalind dressing as Gannymede
Was boy playing girl playing boy;
And when Faustus intones 'Her lips suck forth my
    soul',
It's a bloke who's his Helen of Troy.

With Vesta triumphant as Burlington Bertie,
Reversal rehearsals for Noël and Gertie,
And Charley's Aunt another role we must thank
For ambiguous Shakespeare on the South Bank.

'Cos feminist rationale down at the National,
States that the future has beckoned,
As Deborah Warner reveals from her corner
Fiona Shaw's Richard the Second.

So now transvestite casting's becoming all the rage,
What can we anticipate upon the London stage . . . ?

(To the tune of *They're Changing the Guard at
Buckingham Palace*)

They're changing parts at Buckingham's Palace,
Sweet Lady Anne will be Peter Sallis.
As Tarquin the Tyrant, Madonna has starred,
The Rape of Lucrece was terribly hard:
No phallus!

Sir Ian McKellen looks ever so sickly,
He wanted Doll Tearsheet and got Mistress Quickly,

And critics will ponder for ever just *how* right
It was to put Falstaff in the hands of Joan Plowright.

Dame Maggie's Malvolio's frankly confessing,
She won't be cross-gartered, she'll just be
    cross-dressing.
And Emma's Petruchio will leap from a casement,
To land with a thud on Ken Branagh's replacement.

Ms. Suzman has mastered her Edmund the Bastard,
Cordelia's Peter O'Toole,
And here's Jodie Foster, with guide dog, as Gloucester.
– Lord knows who's playing the Fool!

Memo to Casting Department:
When you are casting the Princess of France,

(To the tune of *Give Peace A Chance*)

All we are saying's 'Give John Cleese a chance'.

For Midsummer sprites in hessian tights,
They went for the Redgraves and got 'em.
And Miriam Margolyes – dressed as a gargoyle – is
Giving her fabulous Bottom.

The casting is final – Titania's fairy
Is played willy-nilly by Julian Clary,
Who was greeted with scorn for his nude
    Joan of Arc,
But hailed by de Jongh 'the best Puck in the Park'.

Here's a fax from L.A. Say – have a nice day!
The Bard by Sylvester Stallone.
He's doing a sonnet in string vest and bonnet –
The Dark Lady with testosterone.

There's a breathless hush as Raquel Welch
Enters up centre as Sir Toby Belch.

And Count Orsino is Rita Moreno,
Shot through plasma by (aagh!) Tarentino.

(To the tune of *Home, Home on the Range*)

Oh give Ian Holm Cleopatra in Rome,
For Octavia summon Tom Hanks,
Cast Dame Thora Hird as Richard the Third,
Alan Bennett can re-write it Lancs –

(*Spoken as Dame Thora*)

'Now is the winter of our discontent –
Them thermal vests are 'eaven-sent.'

(*À la Gilbert & Sullivan*)

If the Merry Blokes of Windsor is getting too
    contentious,
Politically correct but dramatically pretentious,
Then you I shall invite
To a riveting First Night.
Be you ever so misogynous,
There's no sight so erogenous,
Those critics oleaginous
Will find it quite homogeneous:
The RSC presents
At unthinkable expense –
Eddie Izzard's extended opening
As Titus Androgynous.

So bravo, Fiona, your Richard the Second
Is clearly a force with which to be reckoned.
And as for our author, Miss Lipman – oh, why mock?
She's been offered a week in Torquay,
Playing Shylock.

Words by **Maureen Lipman**
Music by **Denis King** (1995)

Stage Directions

'Tis Pity She's the Merry Wife of Henry VI
(Part One)

Act One

Scene One

A certain room in the castle of St. Albans. Flourish. Enter hautboys. A trumpet sounds without. Chambers are discharged within. Alarums and excursions. Enter King with Darlington, Doncaster, Retford, Grantham, Newark, Peterborough, Welwyn, Hitchin and their trains.

Michael Green
From *The Art of Coarse Acting* (1964)

So That's The Way You Like It

JON: And so we bid you welcome to our Court,
    Fair Cousin Albany and you our sweetest Essex
    Take this my hand, and you fair Essex this
    And with this bond we'll cry anon
    And shout Jack Cock of London to the Foe.
    Approach your ears and kindly bend your
        conscience to my piece,

Our ruddy scouts to me this hefty news have
  brought:
The naughty English, expecting now some
  pregnance in our plan,
Have with some haughty purpose
Bent Aeolis unto the service of their sail.
So even now, while we to the wanton lute do
  strut,
Is brutish Bolingbroke bent fair upon
Some fickle circumstance.

ALAN *and* PETER: Some fickle circumstance.

JON: Get thee to Gloucester, Essex. Do thee to
  Wessex, Exeter,
Fair Albany to Somerset must eke his route
And Scroup do you to Westmoreland, where shall
  bold York
Enrouted now for Lancaster, with forces of our
  Uncle Rutland,
Enjoin his standard with sweet Norfolk's host.
Fair Sussex, get thee to Warwicksbourne,
And there, with frowning purpose, tell our plan
To Bedford's tilted ear, that he shall press
With most insensate speed
And join his warlike effort to bold Dorset's side.
I most royally shall now to bed,
To sleep off all the nonsense I've just said.

**Alan Bennett, Peter Cook,
Jonathan Miller** and **Dudley Moore**
From the revue *Beyond The Fringe* (1960)

Mistress Quickly.   Linda Bassett.

Song: *Ladies of London*

ALL: We're ladies of London, as you very well can see,

TEARSHEET: Doll Tearsheet,

COMMON: Doll Common,

OVERDONE: Doll Overdone

QUICKLY: And me.

ALL: Oh well may you ask us just what's going on –
We're off to the funeral of Merry Sir John.
We all clubbed together for flowers for his hearse
As soon as we heard Sir John Falstaff was worse.

TEARSHEET: He promised me money,

COMMON: He promised me gold,

OVERDONE: He promised to marry me when he grew
old,

QUICKLY: He promised to pay and got credit did he

TEARSHEET: From Tearsheet,

COMMON: And Common,

OVERDONE: And Overdone

QUICKLY: And me.

ALL: We're ladies of London and we ought to know;
They don't come more Christian from Bankside to
Bow.

TEARSHEET: He may have been fat,

COMMON: And he was scant of breath,

OVERDONE: But somehow it's 'ard to believe in his death;

QUICKLY: 'Cause all of his life he behaved a bit free

TEARSHEET: With Tearsheet,

COMMON: And Common,

OVERDONE: And Overdone

QUICKLY: And me.

ALL: We're ladies of London, and it won't be the same;
He was sprightly twice nightly, and lord was he game.

TEARSHEET: He owed for his drink,

COMMON: And he owed for his rent,

OVERDONE: He owed for his shirt, but we're sorry he went.

ALL: We'll do all we can for Sir John's memoree,

TEARSHEET: Will Tearsheet,

COMMON: And Common,

OVERDONE: And Overdone

QUICKLY: And me.

Words by **Caryl Brahms** and **Ned Sherrin**
From the musical *No Bed For Bacon* (1959)
Music by **Malcolm McKee** (1994)

Song: *The English Lesson*

ALICE: Ah, poor Sir John, he was a good friend of your fiancé, madame.

KATE: Tell me, Alice, which Henri is it that I am to marry?

ALICE: Why, it is Henri the Fifth of course.

KATE: Hank cinq?

ALICE: Ah oui madame, and he will be here tout de suite.

KATE: Zut alors!

ALICE: Mais oui!

Ma chère madame, today's the day King Henri comes a wooing;
With his atrocious Français, we don't want you misconstruing;
So maintenant, it is le temps to start your English lesson;
We'll learn the names of body parts he's sure to be caressin':

De hand, de naile, de wrist, de foot, de elbow and de fingre;
De shoulder and de waistline where je pense his arm will lingre;
De neck, de chin, de mouth, de teeth, de eyes dat shine like crystals:
De navel and de tummy and de lovely pair of bristols.

BOTH: De hand, de naile, de wrist, de foot, de elbow
and de fingre;
De shoulder and de waistline where je pense his arm
will lingre;
De neck, de chin, de mouth, de teeth, de eyes dat
shine like rubies;
De navel and de tummy and de lovely pair of
boobies.

KATE: Zis English speaking, ooh là là! It seems an
awful menace;
Who wants to learn to talk like people who invented
tennis?
King Henri's hardly chic, why his cheveux's a
pudding basin;
But still, to learn more English words, je connais
I must hasten;
De hand, de naile, de wrist, de foot, de bilbow and
de fingre;
De shoulder and de waistline where je pense his arm
will lingre;
De neck, de chin, de mouth, de teeth, mon Dieu it's
such a puzzle!
De navel and de tummy and de lovely little
schnozzle.

BOTH: De hand, de naile, de wrist, de foot, de bilbow
and de fingre;
De shoulder and de waistline where je pense his arm
will lingre;
De neck, de chin, de mouth, de teeth to smile with
at a suitor;
De navel and de tummy and de lovely little hooter.

Ah, je pense que je suis le bon écolier; j'ai gagné des
mots d'Anglais vitement!

ALICE: Bravo, princesse, c'est magnifique; you now
    need no correction;

KATE: You are too kind, ma chère Alice; I've not yet
    reached perfection;
What is the English money called?

ALICE: It's shilling, pence and pount;

KATE: Et qu'est que c'est, la robe?

ALICE: Oh, Seigneur Dieu, it's called a count!

KATE: Aaaargh!

ALICE: C'est vrai, c'est vrai!

KATE: Aaaargh! Non! Ce n'est pas possible! je ne voud-
    rais pas prononcer ce mot devant les seigneurs de
    France pour tout le monde. Foh! Le count! Néan-
    moins, je réciterai une autre fois ma leçon ensemble:

BOTH: De hand, de naile, de wrist, de foot, de bilbow
    and de pankie;
De waist, de shoulder and de nozz I blow into my
    hankie;
De neck, de sin, de ears, de eyes, de toose inside de
    mount;
De boobs, de tum, de knee, de bum and last of all
    de count.

ALICE: Excellent, madame! C'est vraiment la langue de
    Shakespeare!

KATE: Shakespeare? Merveilleux!

ALICE: Perhaps all the jolie English ladies and
    gentlemen would like to celebrate la langue de
    Shakespeare by joining in with our petit chanson!
    (*To audience.*) Oui, oui?

Song sheet brought in.

KATE: Avec gestures, mesdames et messieurs – garçons
    et jeunes filles – after three – deux, trois, quatre . . .

ALL: De hen, de nil, de whiss, de fart, de bilbow and
de pankie;
De ways, de shedder and de nozz I blow into my
hankie;
De nick, de sin, de ears, de eyes, de toose inside de
mount;
De boobs, de tum, de knee, de bum and last of all
de count.

*Improvise according to response, incorporating a
competition between both halves of audience.*

KATE: Fantastique!

ALICE: Encore une fois! Vitement!

ALL: De hen, de nil, de whiss, de fart, de bilbow and
de pankie;
De ways, de shedder and de nozz I blow into my
hankie;
De nick, de sin, de ears, de eyes, de toose inside de
mount;
De boobs, de tum, de knee, de bum and last of all
de count.

Words by **Adèle Anderson** and **Dillie Keane** /
William Shakespeare
Music by **Dillie Keane** (1995)

The Repertory Actor

The repertory actor earns
  My very high respect,
For think of all the parts he learns
  And has to recollect;
And when he acts in Shakespeare's plays
  His life's an almost hopeless maze.

On Monday, as Antonio,
  He dodges Shylock's knife;
On Tuesday, being Prospero
  He leads the simple life;
On Wednesday he must go to death
  As Lear, on Friday as Macbeth.

At Thursday's matinée he's made
  To play the fool and chaff
As Touchstone, or as Quince he's paid
  To make the children laugh;
At night he must appear again
  To play the melancholy Dane.

Oh, why is Romeo amazed?
  Why does he turn his back
On Juliet, and look so dazed . . . ?

Guy Boas (1925)

Wherefore Art Thou Juliet?

We hear a snatch of the love theme from Tchaikovsky's Romeo and Juliet.

ACTOR: But soft! What light from yonder window breaks?
It is the east, and Juliet is the sun!
It is my lady; O, it is my love!

ACTRESS: The raven himself is hoarse
That croaks the fatal entrance of Duncan
Under my battlements.

ACTOR: (It's not Duncan, dear, it's Romeo.)

ACTRESS: (What?)

ACTOR: (It's Tuesday.)

ACTRESS: (Never mind, carry on.)

ACTOR: She speaks:
O, speak again bright angel. For thou art
As glorious to this night, being o'er my head,
As a winged messenger of heaven.

ACTRESS: Come to my woman's breasts
And take my milk for gall.

ACTOR: (Oh my God.)
I am too bold, 'tis not to me she speaks.

ACTRESS: Come, thick night,
And pall me in the dunnest smoke of hell,
That my keen knife see not the wound it makes.

ACTOR: See, how she leans her cheek upon her hand!
O, that I were a glove upon that hand,
That I might touch that cheek.

ACTRESS: I have given suck.

ACTOR: (For heaven's sake!)

Knocking heard

ACTRESS: I hear a knocking
At the south entry. Retire
　we to our chamber.

ACTOR: With love's light wings
　did I o'er perch these walls,
For stony limits cannot hold
　love out.

ACTRESS: I have given suck.

ACTOR: (I keep telling you, woman,
　this is Tuesday. You give suck
　on Wednesdays.)

ACTRESS: What, will these hands
　ne'er be clean?
Here's the smell of blood still.

ACTOR: Henceforth I never will be Romeo.

ACTRESS: Fie, my lord, fie, a soldier and afeard?

Knocking heard

To bed, to bed, there's knocking at the gate.
Get on your nightgown, lest occasion call us.

ACTOR: I am afeard all this is but a dream,
Too flattering-sweet to be substantial.

Knocking heard

ACTRESS: Wash your hands, look not so pale.
What's done cannot be undone. To bed, to bed, to
　bed.

ACTOR: I have no joy of this contract tonight.

Alan Melville
From the revue *For Amusement Only* (1956)

69

Song: *Cravin' for the Avon*

My poor heart is cravin' for Stratford-on-Avon,
Where all my loves appear in plays by Will
    Shakespeare,
From Caesar to King Lear.

There's nothin' that I wouldn't do for
A nice hunk of man like Macbeth;
Othello's a fellow I'd queue for,
He could just squeeze me to death.
King John is a king that I'm gone on,
For Richard III my heart stops,
With a hey nonny hey, and a hey nonny no,
And Bottom is simply the tops.

CHORUS
Cravin' for the Avon,
Stratford is a haven,
Rantin' and a-ravin',
Cravin' for the Avon.

For an evening with Orlando I would even say
    to Brando
'Call around some other night.'
And I'm sure I'd understand ya better than your
    Queen Titania,
Oberon my favourite sprite!
That wicked first murderer slays me,
Mercutio is ever so cute,
With a hey nonny hey, and a hey nonny no,
And Brutus a beautiful brute.
Ooo!

CHORUS
Cravin' for the Avon,
Stratford is a haven,
Rantin' and a-ravin',
Cravin' for the Avon.

Oh, no!
Shakespeare, Shakespeare give me the works!
Give me the works of Shakespeare.
Cravin' for the Avon, cravin' for the Avon,
    cravin' for the Avon.
Shakespeare!

Words by **James Gilbert**
Music by **Julian More**
From the musical *Grab Me A Gondola* (1956)

William and the Lost Tourist

William wandered home from school, running over in his mind the speech from Shakespeare he had been told to learn by his English master: 'Friends, Rome and Countrymen, lend me some ears, I come to bury Caesar in his grave.'

Suddenly, he spotted a car at the corner of the road, and in the car was a weeping young woman. William stood and gaped. The weeping young woman was astonishingly beautiful, and William, in spite of his professed scorn of the feminine sex, was very susceptible to beauty. William blinked and coughed. The young woman turned sapphire-blue swimming eyes to him and gulped.

'Say, kid,' she said, with an American twang and intonation that completed the enslavement of William, 'say, kid, what's the name of this lil' old town?'

William was too much confused to reply for a moment. During that moment fresh tears welled up in the blue eyes.

'I feel jus' like *nothing.* I've lost the way an' I've lost the map an' I don't know where I've got to.'

'Where did you want to get to?'

'Stratford. Stratford-upon-Avon, that Shakespeare guy's place. If I don't do it today I'll never do it. Everyone I know's done it an' to go back home an' say I've not seen Stratford – well, I'd never hold my head up again – *never –* and I've lost the way and the map and – '

She ended in a sob that reduced William's already melting heart to complete liquefaction.

'It's all right.'

He didn't mean anything in particular. It was only a vague expression of sympathy and comfort.

'You mean this *is* Stratford? Oh, how *dandy*. Do you really mean that?'

Stronger and older characters than William would have decided to mean that when fixed by those pleading blue eyes.

'Yes, this is Stratford all right.'

'Say, kid, I jus' *adore* you. Now I've got to see it *all* jus' as quick as I can.'

She opened the door and jumped down.

'Now the first thing I wanna see is Anne Hathaway's cottage. Would you be a reel cherub, and personally conduct me?'

'Yes, I would.'

William did not repent his rash statement. If this vision wished it to be Stratford it *was* Stratford.

They set off down the road together.

'Is it far?'

'Well, whose cottage did you say?'

'Anne Hathaway's.'

'Oh, no, it's not far now.'

The lady became confidential. She told him that her name was Miss Burford – Sadie Burford.

'I jus' *love* this lil' ole country. I've *longed* so *passionately* to see Stratford; this is the happiest day of my life.'

They turned the bend in the road and there in front of them was Mrs Maloney's cottage. Mrs Maloney lived alone with a dog and a cat and a canary. She was very old and very cantankerous.

William firmly believed her to be a witch. Miss Burford gave a little scream of ecstasy.

'*Thatched*. This must be Anne Hathaway's cottage.'

'Yes, this is it. And there's Anne Hathaway looking out of the window.'

'Does an Anne Hathaway *still* live here?'

'Well I thought that was what you said.'

'But I meant the one that lived hundreds of years ago.'

'She'll be dead by now.'

But if she wanted an Anne whatever it was, she should have one.

'There's another living there now.'

'How *dandy*. A descendant, I suppose?'

'Oh, yes. Yes – that's what she is.'

'Well, will you knock, or shall I?'

'You – you don't want to go *right* in, do you?'

'I sure do.'

'I – I wouldn't if I was you. She's *awfully* bad-tempered, Mrs Maloney is – I mean Anne what you said is.'

'But I must go in – people *do,* I know.'

'But she's mad – she's sort of forgotten her name – she – she sort of thinks she's someone else. It's best from outside. It's not anything like as nice inside as it is outside.'

'But I've known people who've gone inside.'

She advanced boldly and knocked on the door. William stood in the background palely composed, but ready to flee if necessary. The door opened a few inches and Mrs Maloney's wrinkled face appeared round it. At the sight of William it became distorted with rage.

'Ah-h-h.' she growled. 'Ye little pest, ye –'

'Could I – could I just look at your historical cottage, Miss Hathaway?'

''Ysterical yourself, an' me name's Mrs Maloney, I'd have ye to know.'

Miss Burford turned to William with a sad smile.

'Poor woman.'

Then she entered the kitchen. Miss Burford looked round the old-fashioned cottage, the old dresser and the flagged floor with a sigh of rapture.

'How lovely. How perfect. But I had an idea there were more things in it.'

'There were a lot more things, but they had to take them away when she – when she got like this.'

'Eh? What's he saying?'

'Nothing, nothing.'

Miss Burford, throwing dignity to the winds, followed William's already fleeing figure.

'Poor woman. She's sure plumb crazy. But I can say I've seen it now. That's all I wanted to do.'

She took from her pocket a little note-book, opened it and ticked off 'Stratford' and 'Anne Hathaway's Cottage'.

'I suppose there aren't any other of his folks about the place – kind of descendants, you know?'

'There's me. I'm one of his folks.'

He was secretly aghast when he heard himself say that. But he merely continued to gaze at her with his most ingenuous expression.

'Well, now. Isn't that jus' *luck*. You're one of his descendants? *Fancy. Fancy* that. I guess I was lucky to strike *you* first go off. What's your name?'

'William.'

'Of course, after him. Of course.'

When Miss Burford returned home, she gave a little lecture on her English travels. She told of her visit to Anne Hathaway's cottage, whose present occupant was very old and suffering from senile decay. She told how in the same town she met a descendant of Shakespeare.

'It was wonderful, wasn't it?'

Her lecture was a great success.

That Christmas, one Christmas card was sent to William that never reached him. It was sent from America, and was addressed to 'Master William Shakespeare, Stratford-upon-Avon, England'.

Richmal Crompton
From *William The Conqueror* (1926)

Comedy of Errors – R.S.C. Stratford
Antipholus (Desmond Barrit)

Mark Thompson '90

Song: *Teach Me, Dear Creature*

Teach me, dear creature, how to think and speak.
Lay open to my earthly gross conceit,
Smothered in errors, feeble, shallow, weak,
The folded meaning of your word's deceit.
Against my soul's pure truth why labour you
To make it wander in an unknown field?
Are you a god? Would you create me new?
Transform me, then, and to your power I'll yield.

O, train me not, sweet mermaid, with thy note
To drown me in thy sister's flood of tears.
Sing, siren, for thyself, and I will dote.
Spread o'er the silver waves thy golden hairs
And as a bed I'll take thee, and there lie,
And in that glorious supposition think
He gains by death that hath such means to die.
Let love, being light, be drownèd if she sink.

Words by **William Shakespeare**
Music by **Julian Slade**
From the musical *The Comedy of Errors* (1954)

Seeing Stratford

There was one moment in Stratford the other afternoon when I really did feel I was treading upon Shakespeare's own ground. It was in the gardens of New Place, very brave in the spring sunlight. You could have played the outdoor scene of *Twelfth Night* in them without disturbing a leaf. There was the very sward for Viola and Sir Andrew. Down that paved path Olivia would come, like a great white peacock. Against that bank of flowers the figure of Maria would be seen, flitting like a starling. The little Knott Garden alone was worth the journey and nearer to Shakespeare than all the documents and chairs and monuments. I remember that when we left that garden to see the place where Shakespeare was buried, it didn't seem to matter much. Why should it when we had just seen the place where he was still alive?

J.B. Priestley
From *Apes and Angels* (1927)

Anecdotage

There was a woman watching *Macbeth* at Stratford who leant forward, tapping a friend on the shoulder, to say, 'So now do you see how one lie leads to another?'

Another woman, leaving a performance of *Antony and Cleopatra* was overheard saying 'Yes, and the funny thing is exactly the same thing happened to Monica.'

Then there was the experience of Sarah Bernhardt's portrayal of Cleopatra at the end of the last century. This reached a violent and devastating climax in which she tore round her palace, wrecking everything in sight, and finally collapsed amongst the debris littering the stage. The audience loved it and frequently rewarded her efforts with a standing ovation. One night, however, an elderly patron was led from her seat after the final curtain, remarking 'How different, how very different, from the home life of our own dear Queen.'

During an American tour of *A Midsummer Night's Dream,* no suitable theatre was to be found at one of the bookings, so the company performed in a floodlit sports arena. Sir Robert Helpmann, as Oberon, was given the umpire's dressing-room, the nearest the stage manager could find to those usually allocated to the star. When he went round to call the half-hour, there was no reply from the umpire's dressing-room, so he opened the door to check that the actor was there. He was, albeit a little preoccupied.

The stage manager found Robert Helpmann standing on a chair, which was itself standing on a table, craning his face towards the solitary lightbulb hanging from the ceiling as he applied his elaborate green and gold eye make-up.

'Are you all right up there?' asked the stage manager, with some alarm.

'Oh, yes, I'm fine,' said the star looking down. 'But heaven knows how these umpires manage.'

Sir Donald Wolfit's touring company included a young actor whose aspirations sadly outstripped his ability. Wolfit cast him as Seyton in *Macbeth*, entrusting him with the news of Lady Macbeth's demise: 'The queen, my lord, is dead.' He played this for several seasons until it started to bore him and he asked Wolfit for a larger part. Wolfit declined. The actor continued asking and Wolfit stuck to his guns. Into this stalemate came thoughts of revenge. When *Macbeth* was next performed he ran on stage as usual and in answer to Macbeth's question 'Wherefore was that cry?' answered, 'My lord, the queen is much better and is even now at dinner.'

Derek Nimmo
From *As The Actress Said To The Bishop* (1989)

Song: *The Night I Appeared as Macbeth*

'Twas thro' a Y.M.C.A. concert
I craved a desire for the stage.
In Wigan one night, I was asked to recite,
Gadzooks, I was quickly the rage.
They said I was better than Irving,
And gave me some biscuits and tea,
I know it's not Union wages,
But that was the usual fee.
Home I came, bought some dress,
Appeared in your theatre and what a success.

I acted so tragic the house rose like magic,
The audience yelled 'You're sublime!'
They made me a present of Mornington Crescent,
They threw it a brick at a time.
Someone threw a fender which caught me a bender,
I hoisted a white flag and tried to surrender,
They jeered me, they queered me,
And half nearly stoned me to death.
They threw nuts and sultanas, fried eggs and bananas
The night I appeared as Macbeth.

The advertised time for the curtain
Was six forty-five on the sheet.
The hall keeper he having mislaid the key,
We played the first act in the street.
Then somebody called for the author,
'He's dead' said the flute-player's wife –
The news caused an awful commotion,
And gave me the shock of my life.
Shakespeare dead, dear old Bill,
Why I never knew the poor fellow was ill.

I acted so tragic the house rose like magic,
They wished David Garrick could see.
But he's in the Abbey, then someone quite shabby
Suggested that's where I should be.
I withdrew my sabre, and started to labour,
Cried 'Lay on Macduff' to my swashbuckle
    neighbour,
I hollered 'I'm collared, and I must
Reach the bridge or it's death!'
But they altered my journey, I reached the infirm'ry
The night I appeared as Macbeth.

William Hargreaves (1922)

'*More newts – Macbeth is staying to dinner.*'

The Curtain

When the curtain goes down at the end of the play,
The actors and actresses hurry away.

Titania, Bottom and Quince, being stars,
Can afford to drive home in their own private cars.

Hippolyta, Starveling and Flute are in luck,
They've been offered a lift in a taxi by Puck;

And Snug and Lysander and Oberon pop
In a bus, and Demetrius clambers on top.

With a chorus of fairies no bus can compete,
So they are obliged to trudge home on their feet.

It seems rather hard on the poor little things,
After flying about all the evening with wings.

Guy Boas (1925)

Song: *Brush Up Your Shakespeare*

Brush up your Shakespeare,
Start quoting him now.
Brush up your Shakespeare,
And the women you will wow.
Better mention *The Merchant of Venice*
When her sweet pound of flesh you would menace.
If her virtue at first she defends well,
Just remind her that *All's Well that Ends Well*.
And if still she won't give you a bonus
You know what Venus got from Adonis.

And here are some GCSE answers from local schools:
– In *Macbeth* the witches are evil people. They are
   the representatives of Satin.
– Cleopatra ended a remarkable life rather curiously:
   she was bitten by an aspidistra.
– Henry VIII thought so much of Wolsey that he
   made him a Cardigan.

Brush up your Shakespeare,
And they'll all kow-tow.

Brush up your Shakespeare,
Start quoting him now.
Brush up your Shakespeare,
And the women you will wow.
With the wife of the British Ambessida,
Try a crack out of *Troilus and Cressida*.
If she says your behaviour is heinous,
Kick her right in the *Coriolanus*.
When your baby is pleading for pleasure,
Let her sample your *Measure for Measure*.

– In *The Tempest* one of the main characters is
  Prospero, who has a daughter called Veranda.
– Nobody would know Romeo was a Capulet
  because everyone would be carefully keeping their
  faeces covered.
– Some of Shakespeare's plays are written in heroic
  cutlets.
– Shakespeare married Anne Hathaway, but he
  mostly lived at Windsor with his merry wives.
  This is quite usual with actors.

Brush up your Shakespeare,
And they'll all kow-tow.
Thinks thou?
And they'll all kow-tow.
Odds bodkins.
They'll all kow-tow.

Cole Porter
From the musical *Kiss Me Kate* (1948)
Classroom Howlers by children
who prefer to remain anonymous

Curtain Speech

SIR: My Lords, Ladies and Gentlemen. Thank you for the manner in which you have received the greatest tragedy in our language. We live in dangerous times. Our civilisation is under threat from the forces of darkness, and we, humble actors, do all in our power to fight as soldiers on the side of right in the great battle. Our most cherished ambition is to keep alive the best of our drama, to serve the greatest poet-dramatist who has ever lived, by taking his plays to every corner of our beloved island. Tomorrow night we shall give –

NORMAN: *Richard III.*

SIR:– *King Richard III.* I myself will play the hunchback king. On Saturday afternoon my lady wife will play –

NORMAN: Portia.

SIR: – Portia, and I the badly-wronged Jew in *The Merchant of Venice*, a play you may think of greater topicality than ever. On Saturday night –

NORMAN: *Lear.*

SIR: – On Saturday night we shall essay once more the tragedy you have this evening witnessed, and I myself shall again undergo the severest test known to an actor. Next week, God willing, we shall be in –

NORMAN: Eastbourne.

SIR: – Eastbourne. I trust your friends and relatives

90

there will, on your kind recommendation, discover
source for refreshment, as you seem to have done
by your warm indication, in the glorious words we
are privileged to speak. For the generous manner
in which you have received our earnest
endeavours, on behalf of my lady wife, my
company and myself, I remain your humble and
obedient servant, and can no other answer make
but thanks and thanks, and ever thanks.

Ronald Harwood
From *The Dresser* (1980)

THE DRESSER
TOM COURTENAY *as Norman*
FREDDIE JONES *as Sir*

Song: *That Shakespearian Rag*

'Friends, Romans, Countrymen,
I come not here to praise,'
But lend an ear and you will hear
A rag, yes, a rag that is grand, and
Bill Shakespeare never knew
Of ragtime in his days,
But the high browed rhymes,
Of his syncopated lines,
You'll admit, surely fit, any song that's now a hit,
So this rag, I submit.

CHORUS
That Shakespearian rag,
Most intelligent, very elegant,
That old classical drag,
Has the proper stuff, the line 'Lay on Macduff',
Desdemona was Othello's pet,
Romeo loved his Juliet
And they were some lovers, you can bet, and yet,
I know if they were here today,
They'd Grizzly Bear in a different way,
And you'd hear old Hamlet say,
'To be or not to be'
That Shakespearian Rag.

Words by **Gene Buck** and **Herman Ruby**
Music by **David Stamper**
From *The Ziegfeld Follies of 1912*

Song: *Let's Do It*

Mr Irving Berlin often emphasised sin
In a charming way.
Mr Coward we know wrote a song or two to
    show
Love was here to stay.
Cole Porter it's true took a sentimental view
Of that sly biological urge;
But Shakespeare was the first
To really make the whole thing merge.

He wrote that:
Danes do it, Thanes do it,
Sovereigns, senators and swains do it –
Let's do it, let's fall in love.
Queen Gertrude twice in a trice did it,
King Lear evidently thrice did it –
Let's do it, let's fall in love.
We're told that girls dressed as boys do it
Yes, it's strange but it's true;
Henry V did it
With his happy few.
Juliet stayed up late to do it,
Poor Miranda can't wait to do it –
Let's do it, let's fall in love.

In the spring of each year inhibitions disappear
And our hearts leap high.
To Stratford we go (hey nonny nonny no)
With this alibi:
To commune with the Bard in his very own
    back yard,
The temptation is oh so strong;

But before very long
Nature's singing us the same old song.

'Cos leading ladies having flings do it,
Extras waiting in the wings do it –
Let's do it, let's fall in love.
Those handsome leading men do it,
Designers make a model and then do it –
Let's do it, let's fall in love.
Critics in the dark do it,
Then they phone it through;
Box Office staff do it.
No they don't – oh yes they do.
All the names in my black file do it,
One day maybe even I'll do it –
Let's do it, let's fall in love.

Dance Break

Antony and Cleo did it,
Share their loving cup;
Why not head off to The Globe and do it?
And do it standing up.
And now we hope you'll no longer question
The validity of out sugestion:
Let's do it, let's fall in love.

Cole Porter
From the musical *Paris* (1927)
Additional lyrics by **Noël Coward** (1934)
Further lyrics by **Linda Bassett**
and **Christopher Luscombe** (1991/95)

Song: *Put Out the Light*

Goodnight, goodnight, parting is such sweet sorrow,
That I shall say goodnight 'til it be morrow.
Our revels now are ended,
If we shadows have offended
That's all one, our play is done.

Farewell, farewell.
As many farewells as be stars in heaven.
Hence, home, you idle creatures, get you home.
You that way, we this way.
Goodnight, ladies, goodnight.
Sweet ladies, goodnight, goodnight.
Put out the light, and then put out the light.

Words by **William Shakespeare**
Music by **Malcolm McKee** (1995)

Appendix

Part One

Prologue

We first encountered this piece as an RSC voice exercise, but it seems to work equally well as an introduction to the revue.

The Bard of Avon

This is the opening verse of *Brush Up Your Shakespeare*, with new lyrics to establish the premise of the show and lead us into the next item.

Who was William Shakespeare?

This extract is taken from the seminal study by Desmond Olivier Dingle, alter ego of Patrick Barlow and founding director of the National Theatre of Brent. He has said that he hopes it will be 'not only a guide, manual and reference work, but also a deep source of inspiration'.

The Music Hall Shakespeare

A classic example of the fascination which Shakespeare has always had for the popular stage, this song was written by Worton David, whose other successes included *I Want to Sing in Opera* and *Hello, Hello, Who's Your Lady Friend?* The music for the choruses was composed variously by David himself, C.W. Murphy, Harry Castling and Dan Lipton, while the music for the verses was written by Harry Fragson. An Anglo-French artiste, Fragson performed his prodigious repertoire of over three hundred songs at music halls in London and Paris. In 1913, at the age of forty-four, he suffered the unusual fate of being shot dead by his Belgian father, his funeral attended by an estimated

20,000 people. Shortly after Fragson's death, his widow, Alice Delysia, established herself in London as a major star in a string of hit revues produced by C.B. Cochran.

I'm in the RSC!

It should be pointed out that this item is not autobiographical. Jack Klaff appeared in the 1977 RSC Season, not spear-carrying, but playing a variety of substantial roles, and wrote this poem four years later for Dillie Keane, who suggested it to us. It has been performed on many occasions in many versions, usually by women, although it underwent a sex change in our production. Despite his unsparingly satirical view of the RSC, the author did return to Stratford in 1992.

If You Go Down to the Vault Tonight

Mary Holtby is a prolific writer of literary parody and a frequent contributor to the *TES*, *The Spectator*, *The New Statesman* and many humorous anthologies. These two stanzas come from a longer poem about *Romeo and Juliet* to be found in *How to Become Ridiculously Well-Read in One Evening*, a collection of literary encapsulations compiled by E.O. Parrott.

And How is Hamlet?

This sketch comes from the opening scene of Perry Pontac's radio play *Hamlet, Part II*, described by the author as 'a sequel to Shakespeare's *Hamlet, Part I*'. The production starred Harriet Walter, Peter Jeffrey, John Moffatt and Simon Russell Beale, and the script was commissioned by Radio 3 as a companion-piece to the Kenneth Branagh *Hamlet*, broadcast in 1992, just as Pontac's *Prince Lear* served as a prequel to the John Gielgud *King Lear* which was heard on Radio 3 in 1994. Both plays form part of an evening of classical parody for the stage, entitled *Codpieces*.

Moody Dane

Herbert Farjeon was the major revue librettist of the 1930s, and his knowledge of Shakespeare, as a theatre critic and author, perhaps accounts for the series of four *Theme Songs for Shakespeare* (including *Moody Dane*) which appeared in *Nine Sharp* at the Little Theatre. The various characters are portrayed as heroes of the silver screen, this particular number being subtitled 'For a Hollywood *Hamlet*'. With his sister Eleanor, Herbert Farjeon also wrote a number of musical plays around this time, such as *The Two Bouquets* (1936) and *An Elephant in Arcady* (1938). Soon after the Shakespeare Memorial Theatre was built in 1932, Farjeon wrote that Stratford was 'the one spot on the map where you can produce Shakespeare as badly, or as well, as you like and be sure of making a good profit', an idea which the current Board of Governors might question.

Give Us A Rest

Written for a late-night revue at the 1953 Edinburgh Festival, *Give Us A Rest* surprisingly did not survive the transfer to London. In the intervening forty-one years, Sandy Wilson had mislaid the last verse and so has kindly supplied a replacement for us.

The Man Who Speaks in Anagrams

Monty Python's Flying Circus ran from 1969 to 1974 on BBC Television and built on the Oxbridge tradition of satirical revue. This sketch was originally performed by Eric Idle and Michael Palin.

Shakespeare Masterclass

The speech under discussion here is spoken by Ulysses in Act III Scene 3 of *Troilus and Cressida*: 'Time hath, my lord, a wallet at his back, / Wherein he puts alms for oblivion.' The sketch was originally performed by the writers themselves in the 1981 Cambridge Footlights Revue. The cast also included Emma Thompson and Tony Slattery. Probably the most successful Footlights revue since the 1960s, it won the Perrier Award at Edinburgh and was subsequently televised. It was the first revue to be directed by a woman (Jan Ravens) in a hundred years of Footlights history.

The Heroine the Opera House Forgot

This song was specially written for the revue by composer Carlton Edwards and author and broadcaster Laurence Phillips, who have previously collaborated on material for *Déjà Revue at the Afterlife Café* and Julia McKenzie's 1995 *Mercury Workshop Revue*.

Swap a Jest

The 1962 Footlights Revue (directed by Trevor Nunn) featured a parody of modern comics in a music hall setting, and as Tim Brooke-Taylor recalls, the following year this sketch emerged – the same characters, the same clichéd stand-up jokes, but this time translated to Shakespeare's Globe. *Cambridge Circus* was the most successful of all Footlights Revues, transferring to the West End and Broadway. It launched the careers of Brooke-Taylor, Bill Oddie, John Cleese, Graham Chapman, Jonathan Lynn and the producers Humphrey Barclay and David Hatch. Because of its London run, *Cambridge Circus* was unable to fulfil its touring obligations; these dates were taken on by a scratch Footlights company featuring Eric Idle and Richard Eyre.

Which Witch?

This number became a hit for Hermione Gingold, and was revived by her in Alan Melville's series of *Sweet and Low* revues at the Ambassadors Theatre in the 1940s. The Australian composer Charles Zwar came to London in 1937 and began his long revue career at the Gate Theatre before the War. Melville was equally prolific: apart from television and radio credits, he wrote extensively for the stage – musicals, comedies and revues, including *À La Carte*, *At the Lyric*, *Six of One* and a retrospective programme *Déjà Revue* (1974). We found various versions of the lyrics incorporating topical references to Dames Peggy, Edith and Sybil, Winston Churchill, Michael Foot, etc., and therefore felt it in keeping with the spirit of the piece to update it. This was undertaken by Jeremy Browne, a regular contributor to *The News Huddlines* on BBC Radio 2 and understudy in the West End production of *The Shakespeare Revue*.

Away with the Fairies

This lament for five fairies from *A Midsummer Night's Dream* was specially written for us by Dillie Keane (see *The English Lesson*).

Fear No More

Sondheim wrote this setting of lines from *Cymbeline* for Burt Shevelove's adaptation of Aristophanes' comedy *The Frogs*. The musical features a contest between Shakespeare and Shaw, who attempt to outdo each other with quotations from their work. On the topic of 'life and death', Shaw's extract from *Saint Joan* is countered by this version of *Fear No More*. The first production of *The Frogs* was mounted in Yale University swimming pool with an aquatic chorus which included Meryl Streep and Sigourney Weaver. We introduce the song with some further lines from *Cymbeline*.

Othello in Earnest

This Wildean encounter between Othello and his future mother-in-law was commissioned from Perry Pontac (see *And How Is Hamlet?*).

Carrying a Torch

A new song by Anthony Drewe and George Stiles, winners of the 1985 Vivian Ellis Prize for their musical *Just So*. Their other collaborations include the musicals *Tutankhamun*, written when they were students at Exeter University, *The Ugly Duckling or the Aesthetically Challenged Farmyard Fowl* and numerous comic revue songs which they perform as a double act. The quotation from *Julius Caesar* is the Servant's reply in Act II Scene ii to Caesar's question 'What say the augurers?'.

Giving Notes

This sketch was originally performed by Julie Walters in *Victoria Wood, As Seen on TV*. It is a good example of the modern revue style of which Victoria Wood is a leading exponent, chiefly on television but also in a series of sell-out solo tours.

In Shakespeare's Day

This Part One closer was specially written for us by Stiles and Drewe (see *Carrying a Torch*).

Part Two

PC or not PC

Inspired by Fiona Shaw's acclaimed portrayal of Richard II at the Cottesloe Theatre, this is Maureen Lipman's first foray into songwriting. Her Shakespeare career includes an early stint at Stratford, and an appearance as the Princess of France in the BBC Television production of *Love's*

Labour's Lost. Her one-woman revue *Re:Joyce*, celebrating the life and work of Joyce Grenfell (who frustratingly seems not to have touched on Shakespeare in her writing) has been successfully revived for several London seasons. The musical director of this show was Denis King, who will be remembered as one of The King Brothers in the fifties and sixties. He has composed music for over a hundred television series, including *Black Beauty* and *Lovejoy*. His stage work includes the music for the RSC's 1977 hit, *Privates On Parade*.

Stage Directions

The Art of Coarse Acting is one of a series of comic manuals by Michael Green, including *The Art of Coarse Rugby* and *The Art of Coarse Golf*. His *Plays for Coarse Actors* include the Shakespeare parodies *All's Well That Ends As You Like It* and *Henry the Tenth (Part Seven)*. Green took four Coarse Acting plays to the Edinburgh Festival in 1977, and two years later another collection transferred to the Shaftesbury Theatre in London.

So That's The Way You Like It

Beyond the Fringe was mounted as a late-night revue for the Edinburgh Festival in 1960. It brought together talent from Oxford and Cambridge, and transferred to the West End (where it ran for five years) and Broadway. Peter Cook was already established in London as the principal author of the revue *Pieces of Eight* (1959), starring Kenneth Williams. Michael Frayn recalls Alan Bennett telling him that 'they had conceived *Beyond the Fringe* simply by standing round and deciding what they loathed, then sending it up. It sounds almost too admirably rational to be true.' The success of the revue was partly responsible for the craze for satire in the sixties, although this manifested itself more on television than in the theatre, with programmes such as *That Was The Week That Was* and *Not So Much a Programme, More a Way of Life*.

Ladies of London

Ned Sherrin, the doyen of television satire (including *TW3*), directed one of the most successful revues of the seventies in both London and New York – *Side by Side by Sondheim*. He collaborated with Caryl Brahms on a number of musical entertainments, notably *Beecham, Sing a Rude Song* and *The Mitford Girls*. The adaptation of Caryl Brahms and S.J. Simon's comic novel *No Bed For Bacon* has had two scores – the 1959 original by Malcolm Williamson and another by Tom Gregory and John Scott for a revival in 1963. When Ned Sherrin sent us these lyrics he was unable to find either version, hence this new setting for the four ladies of the night, played by both the male and female members of the company.

The English Lesson

This new musical version of Act III Scene iv of *Henry V* puts the songsheet into Shakespeare. Adèle Anderson and Dillie Keane form two thirds of the highly successful cabaret act *Fascinating Aïda*, performing their own distinctive brand of revue on tour and in the West End since 1983. They also have thriving solo careers and Dillie Keane has been a regular contributor to *Punch*, the *Mail on Sunday* and BBC Radio's *Stop the Week*.

The Repertory Actor

Guy Boas was a regular contributor to *Punch* in the twenties and thirties, particularly of comic theatrical verse. In his other life he was Headmaster of a boys' preparatory school in Chelsea, where he enthusiastically produced the annual school play. We have rewritten the last stanza of this poem, which now deals with Romeo rather than Juliet, and thus introduces the next item.

Wherefore Art Thou Juliet?

This is the sketch that has been suggested to us most frequently, but nobody seemed quite sure of its provenance. When we finally settled the matter, the Lord Chamberlain's Collection at the British Library proved inaccessible: the text was locked away in a warehouse in deepest Essex which was undergoing a long asbestos-removal programme. Eventually we transcribed the material from a rare Alan Melville LP. It was originally performed by Thelma Ruby and Hugh Paddick under the title *Yonder Blessed Moon*, and it seems that the present title was introduced during the pre-London tour.

Cravin' for the Avon

The 1956 musical *Grab Me A Gondola* had a long London run starring Denis Quilley and Joan Heal – both veterans of revues at the Lyric, the Globe and the Royal Court.

William and the Lost Tourist

Richmal Crompton frequently refers to Shakespeare in the *Just William* books, and it was difficult to select just one extract. However, this splendid satire on tourism, whilst not obvious revue material, does play particularly well. The prose divides up neatly between a narrator, William, Miss Burford and Mrs Maloney.

Teach Me, Dear Creature

Julian Slade has composed settings for many Shakespeare songs and his version of *The Comedy of Errors*, composed in the same year as *Salad Days,* was the first musical written specially for television. It starred Joan Plowright and Patricia Routledge, later emerging in a stage version at the Bristol Old Vic.

Seeing Stratford

Published in the 1920s, this essay, describing a first visit to Stratford, was reprinted in 1981 with a postscript. By this time, the author had lived in Alveston, a mile or so from Shakespeare's Birthplace, for twenty-five years. This extract was spoken over a musical interlude between the two verses of the previous number.

Anectdotage

These theatre stories, retold by Derek Nimmo in his book *As the Actress Said to the Bishop,* were spoken by the whole company, the apocryphal Donald Wolfit tale leading naturally to . . .

The Night I Appeared as Macbeth

William Hargreaves' song parodies the time-honoured
practice of 'improving' on the Bard (cf. Nahum Tate's
King Lear and *The Music Hall Shakespeare*). In a third
verse (which we cut for reasons of length) Hargreaves'
Macbeth complains:

> The play tho' ascribed to Bill Shakespeare,
> To me lacked both polish and tone,
> So I put bits in from Miss Elinor Glyn,
> Nat Gould, and some bits of my own.

The Curtain

See *The Repertory Actor*.

Brush Up Your Shakespeare

Cole Porter at first resisted the idea of a musical based on
The Taming of the Shrew, although he had frequently
referred to Shakespeare in earlier works. In 1935 he wrote
'As Juliet cried in Romeo's ear, / "Romeo, why not face the
fact, my dear?" ' – the fact being that it was *Just One of
Those Things*. The musical that emerged in 1948 as *Kiss Me
Kate* ran for 1,077 performances on Broadway, making
it Porter's most successful show. In 1987 it was success-
fully revived by the RSC in a production directed by Adrian
Noble. The classroom howlers are genuine.

Curtain Speech

An extract from Ronald Harwood's West End success which
starred Freddie Jones as 'Sir' (loosely based on Sir Donald
Wolfit) and Tom Courtenay as the eponymous dresser
Norman. The play, set in a wartime provincial theatre, was
later filmed, starring Courtenay and Albert Finney.

That Shakespearian Rag

We first came across this song as a reference in T.S. Eliot's
The Waste Land: 'O O O O that Shakespeherian Rag – / It's
so elegant / So intelligent'. Songs like Irving Berlin's

Alexander's Rag-time Band (1911) changed the face of popular music, and *That Shakespearian Rag* was another example of a craze that coincided with the advent of modern spectacular revue. Shows of the period sometimes took their titles from the rag-time songs they featured, *Everybody's Doing It* being a prime example.

Let's Do It

The lyrics for this song have often been altered. Noël Coward wrote new couplets to fit the Cole Porter melody for many different occasions (first recording it in 1934), and we followed his lead, concocting our version for a charity gala at Stratford in 1991. The number seemed a perfect finale to the revue, and we would encourage future casts to slot in topical references of their own. We are slightly ashamed to admit that we used this item as a planned encore, completing the revue proper with the previous item. Coward boasted that he had seen every revue worth mentioning in London, Paris and New York from *Hullo Rag-time!* in 1912 to *Oh! Calcutta!* in 1970. Of his own work in the field, *This Year of Grace* (1928) was, he ventured to suggest, 'the most perfect, the wittiest, the most beautiful, glamorous, funniest revue ever produced'.

Put Out the Light

Laurence Phillips (see *The Heroine the Opera House Forgot*) came up with the idea of a lullaby based on valedictory lines from Shakespeare. The quotations are from (in order) *Romeo and Juliet, The Tempest, A Midsummer Night's Dream, Twelfth Night, Henry IV Part II, Troilus and Cressida, Julius Caesar, Love's Labour's Lost, Hamlet* and *Othello.*

Acknowledgements

We are grateful to the following publishers, copyright holders and agents for permission to reproduce material in *The Shakespeare Revue*. Every effort has been made to trace the copyright holders. If omissions have accidentally occurred, please contact the publisher and they will be included in any future edition.

Bernard Levin for the extract from *Enthusiasms*; Chappells for *Brush Up Your Shakespeare* from *Kiss Me Kate* by Cole Porter; Methuen for the extract from *Shakespeare: the Truth* by Patrick Barlow; Jack Klaff for *I'm in the RSC!*; Mary Holtby for *If You Go Down to the Vault Tonight*; Roger Saunders at Python (Monty) Pictures Ltd. for *The Man Who Speaks in Anagrams*; the Estates of Alan Melville and Charles Zwar for *Which Witch?*; Stephen Fry and Hugh Laurie for *Shakespeare Masterclass*; Michael Green and Sheil Land Associates for the extract from the Revised Edition of *The Art of Coarse Acting* © Michael Green 1964, 1980, 1994, published by Samuel French; Tim Brooke-Taylor and Bill Oddie for *Swap a Jest*; Methuen for *Giving Notes* from *Up To You, Porky* by Victoria Wood; the Estates of Herbert Farjeon and John Pritchett for *Moody Dane*; Warner Chappells for *Fear No More* by Stephen Sondheim; Alan Bennett, Peter Cook, Jonathan Miller and Dudley Moore for *So That's the Way You Like It* from *Beyond the Fringe*; Ned Sherrin for *Ladies of London*; Express Newspapers and The Punch Library for *The Repertory Actor* and *The Curtain* by Guy Boas; the Estate of Alan Melville for *Wherefore Art Thou Juliet?*; Chappells for *Cravin' for the Avon* from *Grab me a Gondola* by James Gilbert and Julian More; Macmillan Childrens' Books for *William and the Lost Tourist* by Richmal Crompton; Julian Slade for *Teach Me, Dear Creature*; Methuen for the extract from *Apes and Angels* © the Estate of J.B. Priestley,

reprinted by kind permission of Peters Fraser and Dunlop
Group Ltd.; Derek Nimmo and Robson Books for the
extracts from *As the Actress Said to the Bishop*; Amber Lane
Press for the extract from *The Dresser* by Ronald Harwood;
lyric reproduction of *That Shakespearian Rag* by Gene
Buck, Herman Ruby and David Stamper by kind
permission of Carlin Music Corp. UK Administrator;
Chappells and the Noël Coward Estate for *Let's Do It* by
Cole Porter and Noël Coward.

Illustrations

We would like to thank the various artists for their
generosity in providing illustrations. Molly Blake, Larry,
Chris Mould, Lesley Saddington and Sandy Wilson kindly
gave us original work. The following allowed us to use
existing material: Deirdre Clancy, Nicholas Garland, Gary,
William Hewison, Gerald Scarfe, Antony Sher, Mark
Thompson, Sylvestra le Touzel and Anthony Ward. The
cartoons by Mel Calman and ffolkes appear by permission
of Claire and Stephanie Calman and the Punch Library
respectively, and the drawing by Arthur Keene by permission of Roger Pringle.